Christian Ethics
for Today

CHRISTIAN ETHICS
FOR TODAY

WILLIAM BARCLAY

Originally published as Ethics in a Permissive Society

1817

Harper & Row, Publishers, San Francisco
Cambridge, Hagerstown, New York, Philadelphia
London, Mexico City, São Paulo, Sydney

Originally published as Ethics in a Permissive Society.

CHRISTIAN ETHICS FOR TODAY. Copyright © 1971 by William Barclay. All rights
reserved. Printed in the United States of America. No part of this book may be used
or reproduced in any manner whatsoever without written permission except in the
case of brief quotations embodied in critical articles and reviews. For information
address Harper & Row, Publishers, Inc., 10 East 53rd Street, New York, NY 10022.

FIRST HARPER & ROW PAPERBACK EDITION PUBLISHED IN 1984.

Library of Congress Cataloging in Publication Data

Barclay, William, 1907–1978.
    CHRISTIAN ETHICS FOR TODAY.
    Reprint. Originally published: Ethics in a permissive society. New York : Harper
& Row, 1971.
    1. Christian ethics. I. Title.
[BJ1251.B32 1984]   241'.043   83-48994
ISBN 0-06-060412-3 (pbk.)

84 85 86 87 88 10 9 8 7 6 5 4 3 2 1

For Jane B and Jane C
who are the modern generation

Contents

Foreword

My first word must be a word of very sincere thanks to the Baird Trustees for entrusting me with the task of delivering these lectures. The Baird lecturers have been a distinguished succession, and it is a very great honour and privilege for me to walk in that company.

My second word must be a word of explanation. Until now the Baird Lectures have been an academic occasion, and they have been delivered to a comparatively limited audience within a college or university. But on this occasion the Baird Trustees and the BBC decided to make an experiment by putting the Baird Lectures on to the television screen. This necessarily altered their presentation. They had to be designed to reach a far larger audience and an audience of a different kind. What had formerly been an academic occasion became an experiment in communication; what had formerly been intended for a limited number had now to be aimed at the general public.

The original title of the television series was *Jesus Today: the Christian Ethic in the Twentieth Century*, and the circumstances in which they were given explain both the form and the subject of the lectures. I am quite sure that at the present time there is nothing more important than the presentation of the Christian ethic. What I have tried to do is to present the Christian ethic in its relevance for today, not in a form for the classroom or even for the pulpit, but in a form which would be relevant and intelligible for people with Christian concern, but with no specialist knowledge. It has been no small problem to do justice to the academic nature of this lectureship

9

and at the same time to meet the need for the wider communication which its presentation on television necessitated. It has been given to me to begin this kind of experiment; I am sure that in the time to come others will do it far better than I have done.

Since the lectures were given on television they were shorter than they would otherwise have been. I have therefore added some material to this book in addition to the actual lectures, and have in some places expanded the lectures. The chapters on the ethics of the Old Testament, the ethics of Jesus, situation ethics, work, community ethics and person to person ethics are the substance of the six lectures which were actually delivered. The chapters on the ethics of Paul, on pleasure, and on money are additional material. This is not a handbook on Christian ethics. Very often subjects which need far more detailed treatment have had to be dealt with in a paragraph. But Christian ethics form a subject on which no book could ever be complete. I have tried to deal with the aspects which I believe to be most relevant for today, and often I have tried rather to open avenues for further thought than to offer any solutions. The fact that these chapters began life as television talks explains too why there is a certain amount of repetition. It could not be assumed that every listener would listen to every talk, and therefore each talk had to be complete in itself, and some things have had to be said twice.

For the Baird Lectures to be put on television was a departure. And this seemed to me to carry with it the necessity of a departure from custom in publishing them also. In former times the Baird Lectures would have been a stately and fairly expensive volume. But it seemed to me—and the Trustees agreed—that the corollary of presentation on television was publication in paperback form.

I have many people to thank for their help and sympathy. Colonel Baird and Rev R. H. G. Budge of the Baird Trust gave me constant encouragement. And I owe a greater debt than I can express to Rev Dr R. S. Falconer of the BBC and to the whole BBC team which produced these lectures on television. He and they combined kindness and efficiency to give me every support.

It is my hope and prayer that these lectures may do something to show that the Christian ethic is as relevant today as ever it was.

Glasgow University,
January 1971   William Barclay

CHAPTER ONE

The Cradle of the Christian Ethic

If you want to put it in one sentence, ethics is the science of behaviour. Ethics is the bit of religion that tells us how we ought to behave. Now it so happens that in regard to ethics we are facing today a situation which the Christian church never had to face before.

Not so very long ago, when I was young and first entered the ministry, the great battle-cry was: 'Don't bother about theology; stick to ethics.' People would say: 'Stop talking about the Trinity and about the two natures of Jesus and all that sort of thing, and stick to ethics. Never mind theology; just stick to the Sermon on the Mount, and let the abstractions and the abstrusenesses and the philosophy and the metaphysics go.' People said: 'Take theology away—I can't understand it anyway.' But thirty years ago no one ever really questioned the Christian ethic. Thirty years ago no one ever doubted that divorce was disgraceful; that illegitimate babies were a disaster; that chastity was a good thing; that an honest day's work was part of the duty of any respectable and responsible man; that honesty ought to be part of life. But today, for the first time in history, the whole Christian ethic is under attack. It is not only the theology that people want to abandon—it is the ethic as well.

That is why it is so important to look at the Christian ethic today, to see what it is all about, and to ask if it is still as binding as ever.

If you are going to understand anyone, you need to know something about his parents and about the home he came from. The Old Testament is the parent of the New Testament and the religion of the Old Testament is the cradle from which Christianity came. It is therefore necessary to look first at the ethics of the Old Testament.

i. The very first thing to say about the ethic of the Old Testament is that it is an *ethic of revelation*.

In this case, if we start out by simply looking at words, then we get off very much on the wrong foot. The word *ethics* comes from the Greek word *ethos*; and *ethos* means a *habit* or *custom*. Are we then to say that ethics simply consists of habits and customs and conventions which have become fixed and stereotyped so that things which were once the usual thing to do have become the obligatory thing to do?

Take another word; take the Greek word for law—*nomos*. If you look up *nomos* in the Greek dictionary you will find that the first meaning given for it is *an accepted custom*. Are we at the same thing again? Is law something which has become so habitual, so conventional, that it has finished up by becoming an obligation? Is it simply a case that the *done thing* has become *the thing that must be done*? Take still another word; take the Greek word for justice—*dikē*; in Greek *dikē* means *an accepted standard of conduct*—and obviously this is an entirely variable thing, quite different in one society from another, quite different in Central Africa and in the Midlands of England or the Highlands of Scotland. Are we back at the same thing again? Is justice simply stereotyped custom, habit and convention? When we talk about ethics, law, justice, are we really only talking about habits and customs—or does it go deeper than that?

In the Old Testament it goes far deeper, for, as it has been put, for the Old Testament *ethics is conformity of human activity to the will of God*. Ethics for the Old Testament is not what convention tells me to do, but what God commands me to do.

ii. Second, the ethics of the Old Testament are rooted in history. There is one thing that no Jew will ever forget—that his people were slaves in the land of Egypt and that God redeemed them. To this day that story is told and retold at every Passover time. 'You must remember that you were a slave in the land of Egypt and that the Lord your God rescued you' (Deuteronomy 7.18; 8.2; 15.5; 16.12; 24.18,22). That is the very keynote of Old Testament religion.

That saying has two implications; it means that for two reasons God has a right to speak. First, he has the right to speak because he did great things. Second, he has the right to speak because he did these great things for the Jews. The Jew would say: 'God has a right to tell me how to behave, for God has shown that he can act with power—and act with power for me.'

iii. For the Old Testament the idea of ethics is tied up with the idea of a covenant. A covenant is not in the Old Testament a bargain, an agreement, a treaty between two people, in this case between God and Israel, for any of these words means that the two parties are on the same level. The whole point of the covenant is that in it the whole initiative is with God. The idea is that God out of sheer grace—not because the nation of Israel was specially great or specially good—simply because he wanted to do it—came to Israel and said that they would be his people and he would be their God (Deuteronomy 7.6-8; 9.4,5).

But that very act of grace brings its obligation. It laid on Israel the obligation for ever to try to be worthy of this choice of God.

iv. Quite often the Old Testament puts this in another way. It talks of Israel as the bride of God (Isaiah 54.5; 61.10; 62.4,5; Jeremiah 2.2; 3.14; Hosea 2.19,20). It is as if God chose the nation of Israel to marry it to himself. That is why in the Old Testament when Israel is unfaithful the prophets talk of the nation going a-whoring after strange gods. Israel and God are married and infidelity is like adultery (Malachi 2. 11; Leviticus 17.7; 20.5,6; Deuteronomy 31.16; Judges 2.17; 8.27,33; Hosea 9.1). It is also why the Old Testament can use a word about God that we perhaps don't much like nowadays

—it talks about God being a jealous God (Exodus 20.15; 34.14; Deuteronomy 4.24; 5.9; 6.15). That is because love is always exclusive. God wants the undivided love of the nation —and if he does not get it, like any lover he is jealous.

Take it either way—take it that God entered into a special relationship with Israel in the covenant—take it that God takes the nation as his bride—either way out of sheer gratitude, out of the obligation that love always brings, the nation is—as you might say—condemned to goodness.

v. I have just been using a word which is a key word in regard to the relationship of Israel and God—the word *chose*. God *chose* Israel. The one thing about which the Jews are absolutely sure is that they are *the chosen people*; that in some way or other they specially and uniquely belong to God. This idea of being chosen has certain consequences—and they are not the consequences that you would altogether expect.

(a) First, it brings a terrifying sense of responsibility. There is a devastating passage in Amos. Amos has been reciting the sins of people after people—Damascus, Gaza, Tyre, Edom, Ammon, Moab—the long and terrible list and to each its doom. Then he comes to Israel—and the feeling is that he is going to say that Israel is the chosen people, and that therefore there is no need to worry; everything will be all right. So the voice of God through the prophet comes: *You only have I chosen of all the families of the earth*—and the hearers are prepared to sit back comfortably—and then there comes the shattering sentence: *Therefore I will punish you for all your iniquities* (Amos 3.2). The greater your privilege, the greater your responsibility. The better the chance God gives us, the more blameworthy we are if we fail him. This is one of the most dreadful *therefores*: You have I chosen—*therefore you will I punish.*

(b) Equally clearly this chosenness must issue in obedience. Moses says to the people: This day you have become the people of the Lord your God. '*Therefore* you shall obey the voice of the Lord your God, keeping his commandments and his statutes' (Deuteronomy 27.9,10). Not, chosen, therefore exempt from obedience; but, chosen, therefore for ever under obligation to obedience.

(c) If then this obedience is of the very essence of life, the law which must be obeyed becomes for the Jew the most important thing in life. As Moses said of the law when he was making his farewell speech to the people: 'It is no trifle; it is your life' (Deuteronomy 32.46,47). The law was that whereby they knew the will of God, and it was through the law that the necessary obedience could be rendered.

(d) This obedience had one obvious consequence—it meant that, if this obedience were accepted, the Jews had to be prepared to be different from all other nations. The word of God was quite clear; they were not to be like the Egyptians they were leaving; and they were not to be like the Canaanites into whose land they were going (Leviticus 18.1-5; 20.23,24). God had separated them from other peoples.

(e) And here we come to the text and the saying which more than any other are of the very essence of the Jewish religion—the voice that they heard again and again said to them over and over again: 'You shall be holy because I am holy' (Leviticus 20.26; 19.2; 11.44,45; 20.7,26). The basic meaning of the word *holy* is *different*. The Sabbath was holy because it was different from other days; the Bible is holy because it is different from other books; the temple was holy because it was different from other buildings. God is supremely holy because God is supremely different. Now the very first duty of the Jew is to be different; he is separated; he is chosen; he is God's; and therefore he is different.

This explains two of the great ethical problems of the Old Testament. There was about the Jews a complete exclusiveness. (There is a qualification of this to come, but to that we will come later.) A Jew was to make no covenant with any other nation (Exodus 23.32; 34.12-15). Intermarriage with persons of any other nation was—and is—absolutely forbidden (Exodus 34.16; Deuteronomy 7.3). Here also we have the explanation of certain things in the Old Testament which have always shocked the Christian—because the Christian so often did not try to understand them. For instance, in war the shrines of any other nation were to be utterly destroyed (Exodus 23.24; Deuteronomy 7.5; 12.3). It is here that we come on that command which is so often quoted against the Old Testament. If a city surrendered, the inhabitants of it were to be made slaves; if a city resisted and was in the end conquered—*you shall save nothing alive* (Deuteronomy 20. 10-18; 7.1-5). Men, women and children were to be obliterated. And so within the nation, if a man left Judaism and became an apostate, he was to be mercilessly destroyed (Deuteronomy 13.12-18; 17.2-7).

Things like that shock us; but just try to understand. At the back of this there was nothing personal; there was no hatred. What there was was a passion for purity. Nothing—absolutely nothing—must be allowed to taint the purity of Israel; the infection must be mercilessly rooted out. Holiness had to be protected by the extermination of the enemies—not of Israel, but of holiness and of God. There is nothing political here; there is no thought of a *Herrenvolk*, a master race who will exterminate other peoples; it is holiness that matters. The day had not yet come—it was to come—when they began to see that the best way to destroy God's enemies is not to kill them but to make them his friends; God's enemies are to be destroyed by converting them, not by annihilating them. But early on the passion for holiness produced the demand for destruction—a demand which is not to be condemned without being understood.

The second ethical problem is to be found in a feature of the Jewish law which leaves anyone who studies it initially amazed. One of the strangest things in the Jewish law is the way in which the ethical and the ritual, the moral and the ceremonial are put side by side. Things are put side by side, one thing which seems to matter intensely and another thing

18

which does not seem to matter at all, and they seem to be treated as of equal importance. Let us take an example; here is a passage from Leviticus:

You shall not hate your brother in your heart, but you shall reason with your neighbour, lest you bear sin against him. You shall not take vengeance or bear any grudge against the sons of your people, but you shall love your neighbour as yourself; I am the Lord.

You shall keep my statutes. You shall not let your cattle breed with a different kind; you shall not sow your field with two kinds of seed; nor shall you wear a cloth made of two kinds of stuff (Leviticus 19.17-19).

This passage begins with one of the greatest ethical principles that has ever been laid down—to love your neighbour as yourself—and it ends with a prohibition of wearing clothes made of a certain kind of cloth—the reason for which is completely obscure. You have the ethical and the ritual completely mixed up.

Now a great many people criticise Judaism because it makes so much of a physical thing like circumcision, because of its food laws, and things like that. But, you see, it is crystal clear that if Judaism had not had these laws it would not have survived at all. The point is this. A good man is a good man to almost any religion or philosophy—Plato, Aristotle, Thomas Aquinas, Immanuel Kant, John Stuart Mill, a Stoic, a Christian, a Jew—all agree on what honour and honesty and courage and chastity are. C. S. Lewis spoke of 'the triumphant monotony of the same indispensable platitudes which meet us in culture after culture'. If it was just a matter of morals there was no great difference in the action of the Greek, the Roman, the Jewish and the Christian good man. What made the Jew stand out, what made him different, is his ceremonial law. You can tell him by what he eats and what he does not eat.

I have told this story before, but it so perfectly illustrates what I am getting at that I tell it again. When my daughter

Jane was young her closest friend was Diane a little Jewish
girl. We used to go out on Saturday afternoons in the car,
and we would stop somewhere for afternoon tea, and when
the sandwiches arrived, Diane would say to me: 'Can I eat
it?' At afternoon tea in an hotel Diane was a Jewess, *and she
showed it.* Would to God we Christians were as willing to
show our Christianity! But the point is that the Jewish
ceremonial law is designed to show the essential difference of
the Jew—it was his witness to his Judaism—and so far from
mocking it or criticising it, it was that, we must remember,
that kept Judaism alive. The Jew has always been the great
non-conformist, for the Jew—all honour to him—is the man
who had has the courage to be different.

We now come to what is the greatest contribution of
Jewish religion to ethics. *Judaism insisted on the connection
between religion and ethics.* This may seem to us the merest
truism, but it was not a truism in the ancient world. We can
see this connection in two things. First, one of the widespread
practices in the ancient world was that of temple prostitution.
The ancient peoples were fascinated by what we might call
the life force. What makes the corn grow and the grapes and
the olives ripen? Above all, what begets a child? This is the
life force. So they worshipped the life force. But, if you worship the life force, then the act of sexual intercourse can become an act of worship; and so temples in the ancient world
had hundreds and sometimes thousands of priestesses attached to them who were nothing other than temple prostitutes.

In Deuteronomy there is a passage like this:
There shall be no cult prostitute of the daughters of Israel,
neither shall there be a cult prostitute of the sons of Israel.
You shall not bring the hire of a harlot or the wages of a
dog (that is, a male prostitute) into the house of the Lord
your God in payment for any vow; for both of these are an
abomination to the Lord your God (Deuteronomy 23.17,
18).

What on earth has the price of a prostitute to do with the temple of the gods? In Greece, everything. In the temple at Corinth there were one thousand sacred prostitutes and they came down to the streets in the evening and plied their trade. In Greece Solon was the first Greek statesman to institute public brothels, and with the profits of them they built a temple to the goddess Aphrodite. The ancient world saw nothing wrong in this. Chastity and religion had no connection. Judaism for the first time made religion and purity go hand in hand.

The second thing that Judaism insisted on was that the most elaborate ritual and the most magnificent church services cannot take the place of the service of our fellow men. What does God want? the prophet asks; and the answer is not church services, but to share your bread with the poor, to take the homeless into your house, to feed the naked. To do justice and to love mercy is what God wants us to do (Isaiah 1. 12-17; 58.6-12; Jeremiah 7.8-10; Amos 5.21-24).

So Judaism insists that there can be no religion without ethics. And that to serve God we must serve our fellow men. As Micah had it, you can come to God and offer him calves a year old; you can offer him thousands of rams; you can offer him tens of thousands of rivers of oil; you can even take your own child, fruit of your own body, and offer him; not one of these things is what God wants—the only real offering is to act justly, to love mercy, and to walk humbly before God (Micah 6.6-8; Hosea 6.6). Once and for all the Old Testament unites religion and ethics, and it did it so permanently and so well that today no one would ever regard a religion as a religion at all, unless it joined the service of God and the service of men.

Before we look at some of the detail of the Old Testament ethic, there are two other general things that we ought to notice.

First, the Old Testament is not in the least afraid of the reward motive. The Old Testament is quite insistent that the prosperity of a nation is in direct ratio to its obedience to God. Given obedience to God, the rains will fall, and the harvest will be sure, and there will be victory over their enemies; and given disobedience to God the national life will fall apart (Leviticus 26; Deuteronomy 28; Leviticus 5.18,19; Deuteronomy 7.12-16; 11.13-17). There are two things to be said. First, the Old Testament had little or no belief in any life to come, and therefore it had to promise its reward in this life; that is one of the differences which Christianity made (Cp. Job 14.7-12; Psalms 6.5; 30.9; 88.5,10-12; 115.17; Ecclesiastes 9.10; Isaiah 38.18). It brought in a new world to redress the balance of the old. Second, there is a real sense in which the Old Testament prophets were right. This much is true—there is not a problem threatening this or any other country just now which is not a moral problem. Industrial unrest, for instance, is not basically an economic problem today; it is a moral problem because—dare I say it?—and to this we will return—it springs from the fact that all of us—I, like everyone else—want to do as little as possible, in as short a time as possible, with as little effort as possible, and to get as much as possible—and de'il tak' the hinmost. You cannot mend an economic problem when the attitude to life of most people makes it insoluble.

The second broad fact to note—and again to this we will return—is that the prophets were politicians. The prophets were not talkers; they were doers. They were quite clear that the only way to turn the vision into fact was through political action. The prophets were the best friends the poor man ever had, and the biggest scourges the rich man ever had. Péguy the philosopher said: 'Everything begins in mysticism and ends in politics.' Of course, a man must have the vision of a perfect society. The demand of the prophet was; 'All right! You've had the vision. What are *you* doing about it?'

So then we come to look at some detail.

i. The supreme characteristic of the Old Testament ethic is its

22

comprehensiveness. It involved every man and covered every action. One of the most extraordinary commands of God to the Jews was: 'You must be a kingdom of priests' (Leviticus 19.6). Goodness, religion, was not the business of a few experts; it was every man's business. Some poet wrote a poem about Judaea in which he said that all Judaea was 'pregnant with the living God'. The writer called Ecclesiastes, the preacher, said: 'He has set eternity in their heart' (Ecclesiastes 3.11, RV margin). All life came within the command and the service of God.

ii. Within the family parents were to be honoured (Exodus 20.12). To strike a parent was to deserve the death penalty (Exodus 21.15; Deuteronomy 21.18-21). If we may digress for one moment—the ancient world honoured parents as a duty which was built into life. The Babylonian code, the code of Hammurabi, has as the penalty for striking a parent that a man's hand should be cut off. Plato laid it down that the punishment for such a crime was permanent banishment, and death if the transgressor returned (*Laws* 881 BD). Cicero said that Solon the greatest of the Greek lawgivers did not legislate for the eventuality of a man striking a parent, for he believed that it was inconceivable that it should ever happen (*Rosc.* 25). Chastity and purity stood very high. The ideal of marriage was high but the practice did not reach the ideal—but of that more later.

iii. There is one very notable thing in Jewish law. The law was specially designed to protect the widow and the fatherless and the poor, for they were held to be specially dear to God (Deuteronomy 10.18; 1.17; 16.19; Leviticus 19.15). But— here is the special thing—the Jews insisted that there must be one law for everyone, the same for the Jew and the resident alien within their gates (Leviticus 24.22). There are two things about a Jew which together make an amazing paradox. The Jew never forgets he is one of the chosen people; he will not intermingle with the Gentile; but at the same time no nation ever more firmly banished racialism from their society. No matter who a man was, justice was his, because God cared for him.

There is only time to dip here and there into the ethic of the Old Testament and to choose some of the outstanding things.

i. To the Jewish ethic business morality mattered intensely. One of the most extraordinary things about the ethic of the Old Testament is that the obligation to have just weights and measures is laid down no fewer than seven times (Leviticus 19.35,36; Deuteronomy 25.13-16; Proverbs 16.11; Ezekiel 45.10-12; Amos 8.4-6; Micah 6.10,11). As the writer of the Proverbs has it: 'A just balance and scales are the Lord's; all the weights in the bag are his work.' Here is the God not only of the sanctuary and the church, but of the counter and the shop floor. The weighing out of the housewife's order and the measuring of the customer's request become an act of worship for the Jew. And that is why I think that it is safe to say that you will never find a dishonest Jew who has stuck to his religion.

ii. One of the outstanding features of the Jewish law is its stress on responsibility. A man is not only responsible for what he does; he is also responsible for the wrong thing he might have prevented and the damage for which he is to blame because of his carelessness or thoughtlessness. If an ox gores someone, if the ox was not known to be dangerous, then the ox is killed and the owner goes free; but if it was known that the ox was dangerous, then not only is the ox killed, but its owner too is liable to the death penalty—for he ought to have prevented the tragedy (Exodus 21.28-32). Palestinian houses were flat-roofed and the flat roof was often used as a place of rest and meditation. So it was laid down by the law that if a man built a house he must build a parapet round the roof, 'that you may not bring the guilt of blood on your house, if anyone fall from it' (Deuteronomy 22.8).

The Old Testament is sure that I am my brother's keeper; it is quite sure that I am not only responsible for the harm I have done, but that I am equally responsible for the harm I could have prevented.

iii. Lastly, there is in the Jewish ethic a kindness that is a lovely thing. A Jew wore only two articles of clothing; an undergarment like a shirt and an outer garment like a great cloak. He wore the cloak by day and he slept in it at night. It was laid down that, if ever he pawned the outer cloak, it must be given to him back again at night to sleep in. And the law-giver hears God say: 'And if he cries to me, I will hear, for I am compassionate' (Exodus 22.26,27; Deuteronomy 24.12,13). The law cared because God cared that a man should sleep warm at nights even in his poverty.

A Jewish workman's pay was no more than four new pence a day. No man ever got fat on that and no man ever saved on that. And so the law lays it down that a man must be paid on the day he has earned his pay—'lest he cry against you to the Lord and it be sin to you' (Leviticus 19.15; Deuteronomy 24.14,15; Malachi 3.5). God cares that the working man should get his pay.

A lost ox or ass is to be returned to its owner, or kept till it is claimed. An animal which has collapsed has to be helped to its feet again (Exodus 23.4,5; Deuteronomy 22.1-4; 21.1-9). In a nest the mother bird must always be spared (Deuteronomy 22.6,7). A field must not be reaped to the edge, nor gleaned twice; the olive trees must not be gone over twice; the vineyard must not be stripped and grapes which have fallen must not be gathered, for something must always be left for the poor and the stranger (Leviticus 19.9,10; 23.22; Deuteronomy 24.20,21). A deaf man must never be cursed and a blind man must never be tripped up (Leviticus 19.14; Deuteronomy 28.18). A man who had just married must be given no business to do and must be exempt from military service for one year to be 'free at home and for one year to be happy with the wife whom he has taken' (Deuteronomy 20.5-7; Leviticus 24.5).

There are few more wonderful ethics than the ethic of the

Old Testament. It has its sternness and it has its severity; but it has its mercy and its kindness and its love. It is the very basis of the Christian ethic, and the Christian ethic could not have had a greater base or a finer cradle.

CHAPTER TWO

The Characteristics of the Christian Ethic in the Teaching of Jesus

The title of this series of lectures is *Jesus Today*, and there are a large number of people who would say quite bluntly that they do not believe that Jesus has anything to do with today at all. The alternative title is *The Christian Ethic in the Twentieth Century*, and there are an equal number of people who would roundly declare that the Christian ethic has no relevance at all for the twentieth century. Are they right, or are they wrong?

You could, if you were so disposed, put up a very strong theoretical argument that the ethics of the Bible in general and of the New Testament in particular have nothing to do with 1970.

i. The oldest parts of the Old Testament date back to about 950 BC; the latest part of the New Testament dates back to about AD 120; that is to say, bits of the Bible are just about 3,000 years old; none of it is more recent than more than 1,800 years ago. How can teaching of that age have any relevance for today?

No one would try to teach doctors today with Galen and Hippocrates as their textbooks; no one would try to teach agriculture on the basis of Varro, or architecture on the basis of Vitruvius. The ancient writers in other spheres are interesting; they are part of the history of their subject. But no one accepts them as authoritative for life and living today. Why then accept Jesus? Why accept the New Testament?

ii. Further, the Bible, the New Testament and Jesus come from a tiny country. Palestine is only about 150 miles from north to south, about as far as Perth is from Carlisle or Doncaster from London. Palestine is about forty-five miles from east to west, less than the distance from Glasgow to Edinburgh or from London to Brighton. How can an ethic coming from a tiny country like that be an ethic for the world? Further, Palestine was inhabited by the Jews, and the Jews deliberately isolated themselves from other countries and other cultures. How can an ethic that comes from a country with a deliberate policy of self-isolation be an ethic for the world? Still further, politically the Jews were failures. They were subject to Assyria, Babylon, Persia, Greece, Rome. They hardly knew what freedom and independence were. How can an ethic that comes from a tiny, isolated, subject country be an ethic for the world?

iii. Again, it is obvious that life in Palestine was nothing like what life is today. Just think. The wages of a working man in Palestine were about four new pence a day. Even allowing for the vast difference in purchasing power, four new pence a day bears no relation to the wages which a man earns in the affluent society, in which people never had it so good. In the ancient world there was no such thing as industry in the modern sense of the term, no factories, no machines, no mechanisation, no industrialisation.

Again, in that ancient world society was by our standards extraordinarily immobile. In the early chapters of Samuel we read of Samuel and his mother Hannah. She took the little boy from his home in Ramah to the tabernacle in Shiloh and left him there with Eli the priest. And then it goes on to say that once a year she made him a new little coat, and once a year she visited him with the coat (1 Samuel 2.19). You would think that it was a tremendous journey, a journey that could only be faced once a year. In point of fact Ramah was fifteen miles from Shiloh! Jesus was only once in his life more than about seventy miles from home. When you think of the difference between that and a society in which a summer holiday in Spain is a commonplace, and a flight to the moon a possibility, then you see that that society and ours are worlds apart.

How then can a teaching and an ethic given in a society like that have any connection at all with today?

Two things have to be said. Firstly, externals can change while the underlying principles remain the same. Take the case of buildings. There is a very great difference between the Pyramids in Egypt, the Parthenon in Athens, Canterbury Cathedral, Liverpool Cathedral, Coventry Cathedral, and the Post Office Tower in London. Externally they look worlds apart, and yet underlying them all there are the same laws of architecture, because, if there were not, they would simply fall down. The externals can be as different as can be; the underlying principle is the same.

Now add the second thing. The one thing that the Christian ethic is all about is personal relationships. It is about the relationship between men and men, and men and women, and men and women and God; and personal relationships don't change. Love and hate, honour and loyalty remain the same.

Someone took this illustration—when Rachel arrived to marry Jacob she arrived on a camel, in eastern robes and veiled and hidden; the modern bride arrives in a hired Rolls-Royce and a miniskirt. But the situation is exactly the same—two young people in love. You remember Thomas Hardy's lines:

> *Yonder a maid and her wight*
> *Go whispering by,*
> *War's annals will fade into night*
> *Ere their story die.*

This is why the ethics of the New Testament and of the Bible are as valid today as ever they were. It is because they are all about the unchangeable things, the relations which do not alter so long as men are men and women are women and God is God.

If this is so, one thing stands out about the Christian ethic—it is *a community ethic*. It is an ethic which would be almost impossible for a man to live in isolation from his fellow men. Love, loyalty, forgiveness, service—these are community matters; things which can only be found and exercised when people live together. When John Wesley was young and still bewildered in the faith he formed a plan to get himself a hut on the moors and to go away and live alone with God. An older and at that time a wiser Christian said to him: 'God knows nothing of solitary religion.' This business of Christian living is something which is to be found among men.

Now we must ask the all-important question. What is it that characterises the ethic of the New Testament? Or to put it in another way in view of what we have been saying— what is it that characterises the personal relationship of the Christian with his fellow men?

This has got to be pushed one step back. We have to ask first—what are the personal relationships of God with his creatures as taught by Jesus? We have to ask that for this reason: one of the main features of the Christian ethic lies in the demand for imitation. Men are to imitate Jesus. Peter says that Jesus left as an example that we should follow in his steps (1 Peter 2.21). The word he uses for example is *hupogrammos*, and *hupogrammos* was the word for the perfect line of copperplate handwriting at the top of the page of a child's exercise-book, the line which had to be copied. So then the Christian has to copy Jesus. And it is Paul's demand that the Christian should imitate God—and after all is this not a reasonable demand since man, as the Bible sees it, is made in the image and the likeness of God (Ephesians 5.1; Genesis 1.26,27)?

So then what we really have to ask is—what is the new thing that Jesus taught about God in regard to God's personal relationships with his people?

If we go to the Greek ideas about God, we find that the first and most basic idea of God is the idea of God's absolute serenity, a serenity which nothing in earth or in heaven can affect. The Greeks used two words about God. They talked about his *ataraxia*. When Jesus talked about our hearts being *troubled*, he used the verb (*tarassō*) which is the opposite of *ataraxia*. *Ataraxia* is undisturbedness; it is inviolable peace. The Stoics talked about the *apatheia* of God, by which they meant that God was by his nature incapable of feeling. It is feeling which disturbs. If you can love, you can be worried and sad and distressed about the one you love. They felt that the one essential thing about God was this serene, undisturbed, absolute, untouchable peace. To have that peace God, they said, must be without feeling.

Here is the difference which Christianity made. Jesus Christ came to tell men of a God who cares desperately, a God who is involved in the human situation, a God who in the Old Testament phrase is afflicted in all our afflictions, a God who is concerned. A detached serenity is the very opposite of the Christian idea of God. The insulated, emotionless deity is the reverse of the Christian God.

If this is so, then the basis of the Christian ethic is clear—*the basis of the Christian ethic is concern*. Here is the essence of three of the great parables of Jesus. In the parable of the sheep and the goats (Matthew 25.31-46), the standard of the final judgment of men is quite simply: Were you concerned about people in trouble? In the parable of the rich man and Lazarus (Luke 16.19-30) there is not the slightest indication that the rich man was in any way cruel to Lazarus. The trouble was that he never noticed the existence of Lazarus. Lazarus was there in poverty and pain and the rich man simply accepted him as part of the landscape; he was not in the least concerned; and in the parable he finished up in hell.

The third parable is that of the Good Samaritan (Luke 10.29-37). The whole point of the parable is the concern of the Samaritan. While the others passed by on the other side, concerned only to avoid all contact with suffering, the Samaritan was concerned and did something.

William Booth would always deny that the vast and wide-ranging work of the Salvation Army was planned. He used to say:

> We saw the need. We saw the people starving, we saw people going about half-naked, people doing sweated labour; and we set about bringing a remedy for these things. We were obliged—there was a compulsion. How could one do anything else?

But the whole trouble is that plenty of people can do something else—they can do nothing. It was this concern that haunted a man like William Booth. 1868 was the last Christmas Day he ever spent in the normal way with a meal and a party. He had come back from preaching in Whitechapel in the morning. He tried to keep Christmas, but he couldn't. 'I'll never spend a Christmas Day like this again,' he said. 'The poor have nothing but the public house, nothing but the public house.' Later in life he was to say when the agony of dyspepsia made eating almost impossible for him: 'They bring me eggs for breakfast and right now children are starving.' What haunted him above all was put in that most pathetic of phrases—he was haunted by the thought of children to whom the word *kiss* was a meaningless mystery.

First, then, the basis of the Christian ethic is the basis of the being of God and of the life of Jesus Christ—it is concern.

In this life of concern the Christian is the very reverse of the Greek. Inevitably the Greek saw life in terms of a God who was serene, isolated, untouchable, freed from all feeling and emotion. Therefore, he argued, a man must be like this. And so his great aim could be summed up in one sentence: 'Teach yourself not to care. Whatever happens, God sent it anyway. Therefore accept it.'

But the Stoics went farther; they saw life as a process of learning not to care. Epictetus gives his advice; begin, he says, with a torn robe or a broken cup or plate and say, I don't care. Go on to the death of a pet dog or horse, and say, I don't care. In the end you will come to a stage when you can stand beside the bed of your loved one and see that loved one die, and say, I don't care.

For the Stoic life was a progress in not caring; for a Christian life is a process of learning to care—like God.

Set that beside the last speech William Booth made in 1912 when he was an old man and knew that he was going to become blind:

When women weep as they do now, I'll fight; while little children go hungry as they do now, I'll fight; while men go to prison in and out, in and out, I'll fight; while there yet remains one dark soul without the light of God, I'll fight— I'll fight to the end.

And he did. If you want to see what the Christian ethic is all about place that dying battle-cry of Booth beside the education in not caring—and you have the difference.

The Gospels have a word for this attitude of concern. They call it love. Since this is at the very heart of the Christian ethic we must look more closely at it.

We begin with a disadvantage. In English the word *love* has a highly emotional content. It is that outreach and upsurge of the heart which we feel for those who are very near and very dear to us. And so when we are told that we must *love* our neighbour, and still more, when we are told that we must *love* our enemies, we are daunted by the seeming impossibility of the task. Love, as we have learned to use the word, is not something which can be diffused over a great number of people; it is necessarily something which by its nature has to be concentrated on some very few, on some one person. The Greeks knew this. They knew all about the love which was a passion and a desire, overmastering in its intensity, and they called it *erōs*. They knew of the steadfast love of affection which comes from the experience of facing life together, the lasting love which binds two people together, even when passion is spent. They called it *philia*. They knew of the love which a child has for his parent, a son for his mother, a daughter for her father, a brother for a sister, a love into which sex does not enter at all. They called it *storgē*.

But the love which Jesus demands is none of these things; it is *agapē*. What is it, this *agapē*? We have it described to us in terms of the attitude of God to men:

You have heard that it was said, 'You shall love your neighbour, and hate your enemy.' But I say to you, Love your enemies, and pray for those who persecute you, so that you may be the sons of your Father who is in heaven; for he makes his sun rise on the evil and on the good, and sends rain on the just and on the unjust (*Matthew 5.43-45*).

What then is the distinguishing thing about this love of God which is to be our love for our fellow men? Its characteristic is that to good and evil, to just and unjust, God gives his gifts. The sunlight and the rain are there for all men. So this means that, whether a man is good or bad, God's goodwill goes out to this man; God wants nothing but his good; God's benevolence is around him and about him.

This is what Christian love is. It is an attitude to other people. It is the set of the will towards others. It is the attitude of a goodwill that cannot be altered, a desire for men's good that nothing can kill. Quite clearly, this is not simply a response of the heart; this is not an emotional reaction; this is an act of the will. In this it is not simply our heart that goes out to others; it is our whole personality. *And this is why it can be commanded and demanded of us.* It would be impossible to demand that we love people in the sense of falling in love with them. It would be impossible to demand that we love our enemies as we love those who are dearer to us than life itself. But it is possible to say to us: 'You must try to be like God. You must try never to wish anything but good for others. You must try to look at every man with the eyes of God, with the eyes of goodwill.'

Luther noticed one thing about the love of God. In the Heidelberg Disputation of 1518 he was talking about the love of God, and he said this: 'Sinners are attractive because they are loved; they are not loved because they are attractive.' God does not love us because we are attractive and lovable people; he loves us as we are, and by his love he recreates us and remakes us. This is how we ought to love others. We do not love them because they are lovable; no one needs anyone to command him to love a winsome and attractive person. The whole point about Christian love is that it is that attitude of the mind and the will and the whole personality which can make us love the unlovely, the unlovable, the unloving, even those who hate us and hurt us and injure us, in the sense that, do what they like, we will never have anything but goodwill to them, and we will never seek anything but their good.

This is the concern of the Christian, because this is the concern of God. It is not a spasmodic emotional thing; it is not something which is dependent on the attractiveness of the other person. It has learned to look on men as God looks on them, with an eye which is not blind to their faults and their failings and their sins, but which for ever and for ever yearns to help, and the worse the man is, the greater the yearning to help. There is a sense in which the more a man hurts me the more I must love him, because the more he needs my love.

Nor is this quite the end of the matter. Luther begins the section of the Disputation from which I have already quoted like this:

The love of God does not find, but creates, that which is pleasing to it. The love of man comes into being through that which is pleasing to it.

This is to say, human love loves that which is lovable; divine love loves that which is unlovable, and by loving it makes it lovable. This Christian love, then, to be like God's love has this attitude of unchanging goodwill, but it does not simply accept the other person as he is, as if it did not matter if he always remained the same and never became otherwise. The Christian, like God, wishes to love men into loveliness, into goodness, into love in return. It does not always work, but sometimes it can blessedly happen that we can love a person out of bitterness and out of hatred and into love. To answer hatred with hatred, bitterness with bitterness, can do nothing but beget hatred and bitterness. There are times when we will fail, but the only way to make the unloving loving is by love. And that is what Christian concern means.

But we go one step farther than this—and again it is the new thing Jesus brought—the Christian ethic is not only concern, it is *universal concern*. I suppose the greatest moral teacher the Greeks ever had was Plato; but you can only describe the ethic of Plato as an aristocratic ethic. He saw life as aimed at the production of the philosopher kings who were, as it were, right at the top of a human pyramid; and the ordinary people existed only to make life possible for the magnificent few. Greek civilisation was built on slavery, and a slave was a living tool.

It took the world about 1,800 years to begin to discover this part of the Christian ethic. As late as 1895 the Salvation Army started work in India and lived among the Indians. An English official said to the Salvationists: 'I don't know how you can bear to live among these people. To us, they're cattle, just cattle.'

That's India. All right, do you know that as late as 1865 in this country only one man in twenty-four had the vote? Just at the turn of the eighteenth century into the nineteenth century the word *democrat* was a bad word. Thomas Coke, the famous Methodist, second only to John Wesley, writes to Henry Dundas:

When a considerable number of democrats had crept in among us, to the number of about 5,000, I was the principal means of their being entirely excluded from our Society.

Did not Queen Victoria herself write that she could never be 'the queen of a democratic monarchy'?

It took the world a very long time to see that the Christian ethic demands not only concern, but universal concern.

But in contrast with what went before there is still something else to say. The Christian ethic demands concern; it

36

demands universal concern; and it demands *passionate* concern.

We have already looked at Plato's ethic. The other supreme Greek philosopher was Aristotle, and Aristotle produced one of the most famous of all ethical theories, the theory of the mean. We would now call it the happy medium. He taught that virtue is always the mean between two extremes. On the one side there is the extreme of excess and on the other side there is the extreme of defect, and in between there is the mean. So on the one side there is cowardice; on the other side there is recklessness; and in between there is courage. On the one side there is the miser; on the other side there is the spendthrift; and in between there is the generous man.

When you have an ethic like that the one thing you can never have is enthusiasm. You are always busy calculating between too much and too little, balancing and adjusting. It is an ethic of calculation. But the Christian ethic is the passionate ethic; it is not the ethic of the man who carefully calculates every risk; it is the ethic of the man who flings himself into life, and whose sympathy with men is a passion.

We have to add still something else to the concern of the Christian ethic; the concern of the Christian ethic is a *total concern*. As Paul saw it, man is body, soul and spirit. The body is the flesh and blood part of a man; the soul, the *psuchē*, is not what we usually mean by soul. The soul is the animal life of a man. Everything that lives has *psuchē*. An animal has *psuchē*; even a plant has *psuchē*; *psuchē* is the breath of physical life which all living things share. The spirit, the *pneuma*, is that which is unique to man; this is what man alone has; this is the part of man which is kin to God and to which God can speak.

Now here again Christianity brought something new into the world. The ancient world by and large despised and feared the body; it thought that all man's troubles and sins and sufferings came from the fact that he had a body. Plato said that the body is the prison-house of the soul. Seneca spoke of the detestable habitation of the body. Epictetus said that he was a poor soul shackled to a corpse. The ancient world hated the body. And there is still a strain in Christianity which is ashamed of the body, a strain which is still frightened of sex and of physical things, and which thinks that things like that are not quite polite and should not be spoken of.

The Christian ethic is quite sure of two things. It is quite sure that we can take our body and offer it as a sacrifice to God (Romans 12.1); that in fact is exactly what we must do. To allow the body to become weak and ill and inefficient and fat and flabby is a sin. It is just as much a sin to let our body run to seed as it is to let your soul run to seed. Physical fitness is one of the duties laid on a Christian.

Second, the Christian is as concerned with men's bodies as he is with their souls. William Booth could never forget the saying of Jesus before the feeding of the five thousand: 'Give ye them to eat' (Matthew 14.16). That is why he started his Food-for-the-Million shops and why he gave men and women free meals. That is why Bramwell Booth was in Covent Garden Market with a barrow at three o'clock in the morning begging for rejected vegetables and bones to make soup. That is why Booth said:

No one gets a blessing, if they have cold feet, and nobody ever gets saved if they have toothache.

Booth knew that men's bodies mattered. George Whitefield was with Booth here. When Whitefield went to America he certainly took one hundred and fifty common prayer books and a lot of books of sermons; but he also took enough material things to fill two pages of print—at random—twenty-four striped flannel waistcoats, twelve dozen shirt buttons; rhubarb, senna, saffron, gentian-root, a Cheshire cheese; three barrels of raisins; pepper, oatmeal, onions, sage and two hogsheads of fine white wine! When he got on board ship he writes in his diary:

The sick increased upon my hands, but were very thankful for my furnishing them with sage-tea, sugar, broth etc.

He reached America and we find him supplying a family with eight sows and a pig; we find him giving a cow and a calf to a poor woman; and barrels of flour to a poor baker. There are times when sermons and prayers and Bible readings are very poor substitutes for a good meal.

We will not forget that the Christian ethic ought never to forget that men have bodies and these bodies are the property of God and that they matter to God.

We have always to remember that the Christian ethic is an ethic which looks to the beyond. It remembers that there is a world to come. That does not mean that it offers pie in the sky; it does not mean that it is so concerned with heaven that earth is a desert drear. But it does mean that the Christian knows that life is going somewhere; that this life is the first chapter of a continued story; and that what happens after death is affected deeply by the kind of life that we live here.

When Dick Sheppard died after his most notable ministry in St Martin-in-the-Fields, one of the great national daily papers published a cartoon. It showed Dick's empty pulpit, and on the pulpit, an open Bible, and beneath, the caption: Here endeth the reading of the first lesson.

The Christian ethic lives in the consciousness of eternity.

You remember the byreman in Stevenson's story. Stevenson asked him if he never got tired of the muck and the mud and the dirt of the byre as his work. 'No,' he said. 'No; he that has something ayont need never weary.' The Christian ethic is lived in the light of the beyond.

It is very important to note that the Christian ethic is a positive ethic. This is to say that the Christian ethic on the whole tells us rather what to do than what not to do.

The Ten Commandments are on the whole *Thou shalt not's*. In one particular commandment—not one of the Ten Commandments—this is of the first importance. This is in what is usually known as the Golden Rule. In its negative form the Golden Rule is to be met with in many systems of ethics: Don't do to others what you would not like them to do to you. But the Christian version of it is positive: Do to others what you would like them to do to you (Matthew 7.12). The Christian version is much the more demanding. It is not so very difficult to abstain from doing things. But the Christian demand is not simply that we abstain from doing things to others, but that we actively do to them what we would wish them to do to us.

This is the Christian doctrine of love. We have to note very carefully the word the Christian ethic uses for love. It is the word *agapē*. It has no passion in it; no sex; it has no sentimental romanticism in it. It means an undefeatable attitude of goodwill; it means that no matter what the other man does to us we will never under any circumstances seek anything but his good. It is an attitude of goodwill to others no matter what they are like. It is not simply a reaction of the heart; it is a direction of the will. It can be exercised even to the person we do not like, because, even not liking him, we can still deliberately and purposefully wish him nothing but well and act for nothing but his good.

The whole point of the Christian ethic is not that it supplies us with a list of things we must not do. It says to us: Your attitude to your fellow men must be such that you wish only their good. And if you look at men like that, then the practice of the Christian ethic becomes the inevitable result.

There is another and a very important sense in which the Christian ethic is a total ethic. It is an ethic of thought as well as of action; of feelings as well as of conduct. Thus it condemns not only murder, but also the anger which brought about the murder (Matthew 5.21, 22). But we must have a care as to just how we state this inner demand, and in particular in one application of it. Jesus said:

> You have heard that it was said: You shall not commit adultery. But I say to you that everyone who looks at a woman lustfully has already committed adultery with her in his heart (*Matthew 5.28*).

If we will only think, we will not say—as some have said—

that the wrong desire is just as bad as the wrong deed. If that were so, we would be saying that it is just as wrong to have a temptation as it is to fall to that temptation. In that case we might as well fall to the temptation straight away. To have a wrong desire and to resist it cannot be as bad as to have a wrong desire and to act on it.

This saying of Jesus has worried a great many people. If we go to the Greek of it, we see what Jesus really meant. What the Greek condemns is not the person who looks at a beautiful person and has an instinctive reaction of admiration and even of desire. What it does condemn—and the Greek makes this quite clear—is the person who looks at another in such a way as deliberately to awaken and to foment desire. What is condemned is a particular kind of looking; the kind of looking which reads pornographic literature in order quite deliberately to waken desire; the kind of looking to be found at a strip-tease show; the kind of looking which, as the French phrase has it, undresses with its eyes the person at whom it looks; the kind of looking which smears anything with a kind of smut and filthiness. This does not condemn the kind of looking which comes to all of us simply because a man is a man and a woman is a woman and God made us so. It condemns the prying, peering looking which uses the eyes to foment desire.

What in the end Jesus is saying in these teachings of his about the inner desire is that in the last analysis the only thing which is truly sufficient, the only peak which is at the top of the Christian ethic, is the situation in which a man has come to a stage when he not only does not do the wrong thing, but does not even want to do it—for only then is he safe.

It is here that we have to look at the phrase which dominates the letters of Paul—the phrase *in Christ*. In Paul's letters everything is *in Christ*. A great New Testament scholar used an analogy to explain this phrase. He used the analogy of the air, the atmosphere. We cannot live at all physically unless the air is in us and we are in the air. Otherwise, we cannot breathe; we die. Just so, for the Christian, Jesus Christ is the atmosphere of his life. The Christian is conscious always of his presence.

We may take another analogy. There are certain abnormal psychological conditions which make a man behave in public in ways he should not behave; and one piece of psychological advice which is very often given to such people is never to go out alone, always to go out with a friend. The whole basis of the Christian ethic is that the Christian never goes out alone. He goes out always with the memory and the presence of Jesus Christ.

So then to sum up, the keynote of the Christian ethic is concern; that concern is embodied in Jesus Christ and is the expression of the very life and heart of God. It is a concern that knows neither boundaries nor limits. It is expressed in the life of the world; and in the world it is purified and inspired by the continuous memory that life is lived in the presence and in the power of Jesus Christ.

CHAPTER THREE

The Characteristics of the Christian Ethic in the Teaching of Paul

Most people think of Paul as a theologian, and a difficult theologian at that. Even within the New Testament there are people saying that Paul's letters were anything but easy to understand (2 Peter 3.16). But for Paul every theological argument ended with a series of ethical imperatives. In letter after letter the theological argument, however difficult it may be, ends with an ethical section which is crystal clear. The argument ends in the demand (Romans 12-15; Galatians 6.1-10; Ephesians 5.21-6.9; Colossians 3.18-4.6; 1 Thessalonians 5; 2 Thessalonians 3). In 1 Timothy the object of the letter is to show 'how one ought to behave in the household of God' (1 Timothy 3.15). The New English Bible margin translation of Titus 3.8 runs: 'Those who have come to believe in God should make it their business to practise virtue.' Paul is every bit as great and earnest an ethical teacher as he is a theologian. Let us then look at the ethical teaching of his letters.

i. For Paul, as for Jesus, the Christian ethic is a community ethic. The great virtues of love and service and forgiveness can only be practised in a society. Involvement, not detachment, is the keynote of the ethics of Paul.

ii. But equally definitely for Paul the Christian ethic is an ethic of difference. Paul's letters are regularly addressed to the people whom the Authorised Version calls the *saints* (Romans 1.7; 1 Corinthians 1.2; 2 Corinthians 1.1; Ephesians 1.1; Philippians 1.1; Colossians 1.2). The Greek word is *hagios*. We have already looked at this word as it is used in the Old Testament of the people Israel. It is the word which in the

Old Testament is regularly translated *holy*, and its basic idea is the idea of *difference*. That which is *hagios*, *holy*, the Sabbath, the Temple, the Bible, is that which is different. So the Christian is first and foremost to be different. That difference comes from the fact that he is dedicated and consecrated to God; and that difference is to be demonstrated within the world and not by withdrawal from the world.

When Paul does not write to the *hagioi*, the saints, the men and women pledged to be different, he writes to the *ekklēsia*, the church, in whatever place it happens to be (Galatians 1.2; 1 Thessalonians 1.1; 2 Thessalonians 1.1). This word has exactly the same implication. *Ekklēsia* is tied up with the verb *ekkalein*, which means *to call out*, and the church is composed of those who are called out from the world, not to leave the world, but to live in the world and its society, and there to be different.

The Christian, says Paul, is not to be conformed to the world, but transformed from it (Romans 12.2). The Christian lives in the world, but it is not on a worldly war that he is engaged (2 Corinthians 10.3). The Christians must be children of God without blemish, shining like lights in a twisted and perverse society (Philippians 2.15). The Christian must not live as if he still belonged to the world (Colossians 2.20).

That last demand brings us to another of Paul's consistent demands. He is always urging on his people that they should make it clear that they are changed, that they have left their old life behind them, and that they have genuinely embarked on the new way. They must no longer live as the Gentiles do (Ephesians 4.17-24). Once they were in darkness, now they are in light, and their conduct must show it (Ephesians 5.8). Once they were hostile to God and estranged from him; now they are reconciled to him (Colossians 1.21-23). Once they were dead in trespasses; now they are gloriously alive (Colossians 2.13). They must put away the conduct which was formerly characteristic of their lives (Colossians 3.7-10). They must not act with the passion of lust of heathen who do not know God (1 Thessalonians 4.5).

It would never have occurred to Paul that it would have been impossible to distinguish between the Christian and the non-Christian. He would have agreed with Richard Glover, who said that there was no such thing as secret discipleship, for either the secrecy killed the discipleship or the discipleship killed the secrecy. For the Christian every moment of life was to be a demonstration that he was a Christian.

How does that work out today? In the present situation a man does not come out of a heathen society into a Christian society, for even when the church is disregarded or ignored, the principles on which society is built are now Christian principles. What should happen now is this. Nowadays a man knows very well what the Christian ethic demands. When he becomes a pledged follower of Jesus Christ, he should move from a theoretical awareness of the Christian ethic to a committed practice of it. Knowledge should turn into action—whatever the cost.

iii. The idea of difference can be taken a step farther and confront us with something of a problem. There are times in Paul's teaching when the difference turns into severance. There are times in Paul's letters when the difference seems to become segregation. In 2 Corinthians 6.14-16 Paul writes: 'Do not be mismated with unbelievers. For what partnership have righteousness and iniquity? Or what fellowship has light with darkness? What accord has Christ with Belial? Or what has a believer in common with an unbeliever?' The Letter to the Ephesians speaks of those who are immoral and impure, and then goes on to say: 'Do not associate with them' (Ephesians 5.7). Paul warns the Thessalonians to keep away from any brother who is living in idleness. If anyone will not accept his authority, the Thessalonians are to note that man and to have nothing to do with him (2 Thessalonians 3.6,14). The Pastoral Letters speak of those whose religion is only a name, and whose profligate lives deny their profession. 'Avoid such people' (2 Timothy 3.1-5). If a man is factious, he is to be admonished once or twice. If the warning is ineffective, 'Have nothing more to do with him, knowing that such a person is perverted and sinful' (Titus 3.10,11).

This is a formidable series of warnings. What is to happen to missionary work? Are certain people to be abandoned as hopeless? Is the sinner to be left to his sin? This is clearly something which demands thinking about. Certain points can be made.

(a) We must never forget the general situation. When Paul was writing, the Christian church was no more than a little island in a surrounding sea of paganism. The tempting and the infecting influences were terrifyingly near. These Christians in the early church were only one remove from paganism, and relapse was so desperately easy.

We can see the thing coming to a head in 1 Corinthians chapters 8 to 10. There the point at issue is whether or not a Christian can eat meat that has been offered to an idol, that is, meat which has formed part of a heathen sacrifice. The problem arose in this way. In the ancient world it was only in the very rarest cases that a sacrifice was burned entire. In by far the greater number of cases only a token part of the sacrifice was burned on the altar, sometimes no more than a few hairs cut from the forehead of the beast. Part of the meat then became the perquisite of the priests, and part was returned to the worshipper. With his part the worshipper gave a feast, a party, a celebration for his friends. And—and here is the point—that feast was given in a temple. Just as we might give a party in an hotel or restaurant or club, so the Greek gave it in the temple of his god. The invitation would run: 'I invite you to dine with me on such and such a date and at such and such a time at the table of our Lord Serapis,' Serapis being the host's favourite god. Could the Christian go to such a party? Paul is clear that he cannot. Paul is clear that no man can be a guest at the table of Jesus Christ and then a guest at the table of Serapis. He cannot have it both ways. He must be off with the old love before he is on with the new (1 Corinthians 10.21,22). To try to act like this was to court infection. It could mean that a man's social life came to an abrupt end, but that was part of the price that he had to pay for being a Christian.

(b) The second thing that emerges when we consider these passages is that the person who is being condemned is the person who is deliberately and open-eyed flirting with temptation. What is being insisted on by Paul is that in that precarious situation no man should voluntarily go into company which would endanger his life as a Christian.

(c) And most of all it is the misguided Christian brother who is to be avoided. It is not a case of the Christian cutting himself off from the world and from all the missionary opportunities life in the world gave him; it is a question of cutting himself off from the Christian brother who was hell-bent on folly. Paul makes this quite clear in 1 Corinthians 5.9-13. In the church at Corinth there was a man who had been guilty of sexual misconduct with his step-mother, conduct which would have shocked a heathen, let alone a Christian. Paul insists that the congregation must take action. The man must be ejected. They are not to associate with immoral men. But, says Paul, this does not mean out in the world, or they would have to leave the world altogether. It is not outsiders they are to judge; it is their own members; and if a man claims the name of brother and behaves shamelessly, he must go.

From this certain things emerge. It is the pledged Christian who is in question. The church dare not adopt an easy-going attitude to the man who is guilty of flagrant misconduct. It is a matter of discipline, and Paul holds that if a pledged Christian refuses to accept the ethical standards of the church, then the church must in self-defence take action.

(d) But that is not the end of the story. It is discipline that is in question. Even if excommunication means apparently delivering a man to Satan, the ultimate end is to save his soul alive (1 Corinthians 5.5), and in one case at least we find Paul pleading for the receiving back of the sinner into the fellowship before his spirit is altogether broken (2 Corinthians 2.5-11). The whole process is for cure and not for destruction.

What it all means is that the church cannot continue to be the church and refuse to exercise discipline. The Christian is a man under pledge, a pledge voluntarily given, and he cannot with impunity deliberately break his pledge. And the word *deliberately* is to be stressed. All the way through it is clear that Paul is not thinking of the man who on the impulse is swept into sin and who has never ceased to repent. He is thinking of the man who, deaf to appeal and blind to duty and oblivious to love, has callously and deliberately gone his own way.

iv. A community ethic is bound to be an ethic of responsibility. The Christian is characteristically the responsible man.

(a) The Christian is responsible to the society of which he forms a part. Here Paul uses an analogy which many of the classical writers had used before him, the analogy of the body. The most famous instance of it in the classical writers is in the parable of Menenius Agrippa (Livy 2.32). There was an occasion in Rome when there was a split between the common people and the aristocrats. The split grew so wide that the common people marched out and withdrew from the city. The life of the city came to a standstill. So the rulers of the city sent an orator called Menenius Agrippa out to the people to see if he could persuade them to return. He told them a parable which ran something like this. There came a time when the members of the body grew very annoyed with the stomach. There the stomach sat, they said, doing nothing, and they had all to labour and to combine in bringing food to the stomach which itself did nothing to procure it. So the members of the body decided that they would no longer bring food to the stomach; the hands would not lift it to the mouth; the teeth would not chew it; the throat would not swallow it; and by this they hoped to have their revenge on the stomach. But the only result was that the whole body was in danger of starving to death, and thus the members of the body learned that the only way in which the body can maintain its health and well-being is for every part of it to do its share, and not to be envious and jealous of any other part.

This is exactly the picture that Paul uses in Romans 12.3-8. They are one body in Christ, and each a member of the body. Grace has given them different gifts and all these gifts must be used for the good of the whole. 'No man is an Island, entire of itself,' as John Donne said. No man lives to himself and no man dies to himself (Romans 14.7). We are, in the vivid Old Testament phrase, bound up in the bundle of life (1 Samuel 25.29). A man cannot do without society, and society cannot do without him. If a person 'drops out' from society, he does not really do so. He withdraws himself and his labour and his contribution from society, but if he is to live and eat he has to take what society still gives him. He has chosen to retain his rights and to abdicate from his responsibilities.

(b) The Christian has a responsibility to the weaker brother. He is well aware that he is his brother's keeper. This is true both mentally and physically. What may be perfectly safe for one person may be highly dangerous for another. Paul reminds us that arguments and debates which may be for one man a pleasant mental hike or an intellectual stimulus may be for another man the ruin of his faith (Romans 14.1). And the strong must always bear with the weak, for we are in this world, not to please ourselves, but to strengthen our neighbour (Romans 15.1,2). A man must always remember the effect on others of that which he allows himself. Twice Paul lays this down most practically and explicitly. 'It is right not to eat meat or drink wine or do anything that makes your brother stumble' (Romans 14.13-21). 'If food is a cause of my brother's falling, I will never eat meat, lest I cause my brother to fall' (1 Corinthians 8.13). Saul Kane in John Masefield's poem *The Everlasting Mercy* was haunted by 'the harm I've done by being me'. The New Testament is quite clear that the

Christian must always ask not only: 'What will this do to me?' but also: 'What will this do to the brother who is not as strong as I am?'

(c) The Christian has a responsibility to the state, but that we will leave for future discussion, when we come to talk about the Christian and the community.

(d) The Christian has a responsibility to the man who is going astray. He must gently restore him to the right way (Galatians 6.5). The Christian is conscious of the sin of looking on; he knows that a man can sin just as badly by doing nothing as by doing something.

(e) Three times in the New Testament there is laid down the simple, human duty of providing hospitality for the traveller and the stranger (Hebrews 13.2; 1 Peter 4.9; Romans 12.13). 'Practise hospitality,' says Paul. And little wonder. In the ancient world inns were notoriously bad. In his *Pagan Background of Early Christianity* W. R. Halliday has a vivid chapter on 'Communications' in which he describes travel. He cites a charming but very apocryphal story from the apocryphal *Acts of John* (M. R. James, *The Apocryphal New Testament*, p. 242). John and his disciples came to a deserted inn and settled down for the night. The bed proved to be infested with bugs. Whereupon John addressed them: 'I say unto you, O bugs, behave yourselves one and all, and leave your abode for the night and remain quiet in the one place, and keep your distance from the servants of God.' On the next morning when the servants opened the door 'we saw at the door of the house which we had taken a great number of bugs standing.' John then 'sat up on the bed and looked at them and said: "Since you have well behaved yourselves in hearkening to my rebuke, come into your place." And when he had said this, and risen from the bed, the bugs running from the door hastened to the bed and disappeared into the joints.' The innkeeper's terms were extortionate. Seneca writes (*On Benefits* 6.15): 'How glad we are at the sight of shelter in a desert, a roof in the storm, a bath or a fire in the cold—and how dear they cost in inns.' Many of the inns in the cities were no better than brothels, although of course in the great resorts there were palatial inns for the wealthy; but few Christians were wealthy. So the simple duty of keeping open door for the young person away from home and for the stranger in a strange place is a part of the Christian ethic.

(f) The Christian has a responsibility to Jesus Christ. The church is the body of Christ (1 Corinthians 12.27; Ephesians 1.22). That phrase may mean many things; but it means one simple and practical thing. Jesus is no longer here in the body; he is here in the Spirit. But that means that, if he wants something done, he has to get a man or a woman to do it for him. There is a helplessness of Jesus as well as a power of Jesus. Nothing can teach his children unless a man or woman will do it for him. The help which he wishes the aged, the weak, the suffering, the sorrowing to have must come through human means. He needs men to be hands to work for him, mouths to speak for him, feet to run on his errands. The Christian cannot forget his responsibility to Jesus Christ. It is no small part of the Christian ethic that the Christian is the representative of Jesus Christ.

v. The Pauline ethic is an ethic of body, soul and spirit. It is quite convinced of the importance of the body. The body can be presented as a living sacrifice to God (Romans 12.1). The body is nothing less than the temple in which the Holy Spirit can dwell (1 Corinthians 3.16; 6.19). The body can therefore neither be despised nor misused. It must be used for what it is, and the Pauline ethic has no use for the asceticism which despises marriage and refuses the good gifts of God (1 Timothy 4.1-5). This is in line with Judaism, for there is a rabbinic saying that a man will have to give account for every good thing that he might have enjoyed and did not enjoy.

This has to be seen against a background of Gnosticism. Gnosticism was a type of thought very prevalent in the time of the New Testament. It had not yet developed into the elaborate systems into which it later flowered, but it was deeply ingrained into Greek thought. It came from a desire to explain whence came the sin and the sorrow and the suffering of this world. It began with the principle that from all eternity there have been two principles—spirit and matter. God is spirit and spirit is altogether good. Matter was there from the very beginning, and matter is the stuff out of which the universe is created. But—and here is the essential point—the Gnostic believed that from the beginning matter is essentially flawed; it is evil; the universe is made out of bad stuff. But if matter is bad, then the God who is altogether pure spirit cannot touch it. The real and the true God cannot be the creator. So, according to the Gnostic belief, the true God put forth a series of emanations, each one farther from himself, each one more ignorant of himself, and in the end culminating in an emanation who was not only ignorant of, but hostile to, the real God. It was this distant, ignorant, hostile emanation who was the creator. There is only one conclusion to be drawn from all this—that the body and all that has to do with it is essentially bad. And that gives rise to two possible ways of life. The one way demands complete asceticism, where a man despises and neglects the body and stifles all its instincts and impulses. For him, sex, marriage, everything that has to do with the body is incurably evil and must be abandoned. The second way argues that, since the body is in any event evil, it does not matter what you do with it. Let it have its way; sate its impulses and glut its appetites. It does not matter what happens to it. This leads to complete immorality and to the abandonment of life to life's physical instincts. As Augustine said, he could find parallels in the Greek philosophers for everything in the Bible except the words: 'The Word became flesh' (John 1.14). Flesh, a body, was the one thing that God could never take upon himself.

This is far from the thought of Paul. But it did deeply affect Christian thinking. And the matter was complicated by a misunderstanding of the Pauline use of the word *flesh*. In Paul *flesh* does not mean the *body*. When Paul speaks of sins of the flesh he is far from meaning only physical and sexual sins. Sins of the flesh include strife, jealousy, anger, dissension, party spirit, envy (Galatians 5.20,21). What Paul means by the *flesh* is human nature apart from God. It is what man has made himself in contrast with what God meant him to be. But from the beginning this was misunderstood, and the feeling has lingered on that the body and its desires are something to be regretted, that sex is something dirty and something to be ashamed of, that the instincts of the body are something over which a veil must be drawn. It has been this which has been the cause of that sexual ignorance which has brought sorrow and disaster to so many, and which has put a muzzle on things like proper sex education.

The Christian ethic accepts the body and all that has to do with the body. The Christian ethic believes that the body is God's, and that we can dedicate it to God just as much as we can dedicate heart and mind to him.

vi. The Christian ethic is an ethic which goes beyond this world and beyond time. For the Christian life is lived out against a background of eternity.

(a) The Christian ethic is a resurrection ethic. It is quite clear that, wherever Paul started out to preach, he finished up with preaching the risen Christ (Acts 13.30-37; 17.18,31). All life is lived in the presence of the Risen Lord. All life is meant to stand the scrutiny of his eye.

(b) The Christian ethic is an ethic of judgment. As Paul saw it, all life is on the way to judgment. The destination of every man is the judgment seat of God and Jesus (Romans 14.10-12; 2 Corinthians 5.10). Anyone who continues to be guilty of the sins of the flesh will not inherit the kingdom of God (Galatians 5.21). What a man sows he will reap (Galatians 6.7,8). To be disobedient is to be doomed to the wrath of God (Ephesians 5.6). To continue to live a life of immorality and impurity is to incur the wrath of God (Colossians 3.6).

To remove the idea of judgment from Christianity is to

emasculate it. No honest presentation of Christianity can remove from it the ultimate threat.

(c) The Christian ethic as Paul presented it is never allowed to forget the coming again in judgment and in glory of Jesus Christ. The New Testament is peopled by men and women who are waiting. Nothing must be allowed to interfere with the intensity of that expectation, not even the closest relationships of life (1 Corinthians 7.25-35). The Christians wait for their blessed hope (Titus 2.13). There comes a day, and the Christian must so live that that day will not surprise and shock him (1 Thessalonians 5.2-7, 23; Philippians 2.16; 3.20; Colossians 3.4; 2 Thessalonians 1.5-10). It may be that that coming is long delayed, but however long it is delayed, it does not alter the basic fact that the Christian, as Cullmann put it, is always living in the space between the *already* and the *not yet*. The Christian is the man for whom something has happened, and for whom something has still to happen.

It is clear that all these things will have a tremendous ethical effect. To live in the presence of Christ, to see in life a journey to judgment, to rejoice in the *already* and at the same time to expect the *not yet*—these are things which are bound to give life a certain quality, and a certain ethical strenuousness, which can never be forgotten.

vii. For Paul the Christian ethic is an ethic of imitation.

(a) To begin with the highest form of it, the Christian is called upon to do no less than to imitate God. 'Be imitators of God,' says the Letter to the Ephesians, 'as beloved children' (Ephesians 5.1). Startling as this may sound, it is a summons to which man is called by the great teachers of both Greece and Israel. Plato says in the *Theaetetus* (176) that a man ought to fly away from this earth to heaven as quickly as possible, and to fly away is to become like God, so far as this is possible for a man. Before Plato, Pythagoras had taken as his maxim: 'Follow God.'

The same idea was there in Jewish thought. In the second

series of *Studies in Pharisaism and the Gospels* Israel Abrahams has an essay on 'The Imitation of God'. There he quotes from one of his best loved books, a Jewish classical devotional work by Cordovero, called *Deborah's Palm Tree*. The book begins: 'Man must liken himself to his Master.' Cordovero then quotes Micah 7.18-20:

> Who is a God like unto thee, that pardoneth iniquity, and passeth by the transgression of the remnant of his heritage? He retaineth not his anger for ever, because he delighteth in mercy. He will turn again and have compassion on us; he will tread our iniquities under foot: and thou wilt cast all their sins into the depths of the sea. Thou wilt perform the truth to Jacob, and the mercy to Abraham, which thou hast sworn to our fathers from the days of old.

Abrahams tells us that in that passage Cordovero sees the thirteen divine attributes, every one of which man must copy. 'He takes the clauses one by one, explains God's method, and then calls on his reader to go and do likewise. Thus man must bear insult; must be limitless in love, finding in all men the object of his deep and inalienable affection; he must overlook wrongs done to him, and never forget a kindness. Cordovero insists again and again on this divine patience and forbearance, on God's passing over man's many sins and on his recognition of man's occasional virtues. So must man act. He must temper his justice with mercy, must be peculiarly tender to the unworthy. His whole being must be attuned to God's being. His earthly eye must be open to the good in all men, as is the heavenly eye; his earthly ear must be deaf to the slanderers and the foul, just as the heavenly ear is receptive only of the good. For God loves all men whom he has made in his very image, and how shall man hate what God loves?' (I. Abrahams, *Studies in Pharisaism and the Gospels*, second series, pp. 145, 146). Abrahams goes on to tell how the Talmud (*Sota* 14 a) on Deuteronomy 13.4 calls on man to imitate God who clothed the naked (Adam and Eve), who visited the sick (Abraham), and who buried the dead (Moses).

'Thus the whole *torah* (the law) from Genesis to Deuteronomy bids Israel imitate God.'

To talk of man imitating God is neither blasphemous nor impossible, for God made man in his own image (Genesis 1.26,27), and the imitation of God is therefore the very function of manhood.

(b) The Christian must imitate Jesus Christ. He can be said to learn Christ (Ephesians 4.20). The Christian is the follower of Jesus.

(c) The Christian is urged to imitate the heroic figures of the faith. The writer to the Hebrews commands his readers to remember their leaders. 'Consider the outcome of their life, and imitate their faith' (Hebrews 13.7). They are to be imitators of 'those who through faith and patience received the promises' (Hebrews 6.12). Paul praises the Thessalonians because in their suffering for their faith they became imitators of the churches of Judaea who suffered before them (1 Thessalonians 2.14).

This is why a man should know something of the history of his church. This is why Oliver Cromwell, when he was arranging for the education of his son Richard, said: 'I would have him know a little history.' History, as it has been said, is 'philosophy teaching by examples'. This was indeed the very aim and object of the ancient historians. It was the aim of Thucydides not to compose a book which was a prize essay, but which would abide for all time, so that, when the same kind of events happened again, as he was certain they would, men would find guidance for the present from the examples of the past (Thucydides 1.22). Lucian in his essay on *How History ought to be Written* (44) says that the historians must above all aim at accuracy and usefulness, so that, when similar events occur and similar circumstances arise, the record of the past may teach us how to act in the present. Livy in his *Preface* writes: 'This is the most wholesome and faithful effect of the study of history; you have in front of you real examples of every kind of behaviour, real examples embodied in most conspicuous form; from these you can take, both for yourself and the state, ideals at which to aim; you can learn also what to avoid because it is impious either in its conception or in its issue.'

A. L. Rowse, a modern historian, makes exactly the same claim. For him the prime use of history is that 'it enables you to understand, better than any other discipline, the public events, affairs and trends of your time. . . . History is about human society, its story and how it has come to be what it is; knowing what societies have been like in the past and their evolution will give you the clue to the factors that operate in them, the currents and forces that move them, the motives and conflicts, both general and personal, that shape events' (A. L. Rowse, *The Use of History*, p. 16). By the study of the examples of the past we gain guidance for the present.

The Christian must know the history of his church that he may imitate its heroisms and avoid its mistakes.

(d) But by far Paul's most astonishing invitation to imitation is his repeated invitation to his converts to imitate himself. 'I urge you,' he writes to the Corinthians, 'be imitators of me' (1 Corinthians 4.16). Again he writes to the same people: 'Be imitators of me, as I am of Christ' (1 Corinthians 11.1). 'Brethren,' he writes to the Philippians, 'join in imitating me' (Philippians 3.17). Again he writes to them: 'What you have learned and received and heard in me do'(Philippians 4.9). He writes to the Thessalonians: 'You became imitators of us and the Lord' (1 Thessalonians 1.6). 'You yourselves know you ought to imitate me,' he writes again to them. His life and work in Thessalonica were designed 'to give you in your conduct an example to imitate' (2 Thessalonians 3.7,9). (This is to some extent obscured in the Authorised Version which translates *mimeisthai* by *to follow* rather than *to imitate*; it is from *mimeisthai* that the English word *to mimic* is derived.)

There are any number of preachers and teachers who can say: 'I can *tell* you what to do.' There are few who can say: 'I can *show* you what to do.' There are any number who can say:

'Listen to my words.' There are few who can say: 'Follow my example.' It was Paul's astonishing claim that he taught by being, even more than he taught by speaking or by writing.

viii. The Christian ethic demands that all Christians should not only accept an example to imitate but should also provide an example to imitate. It has been well said that 'everyone pipes for the feet of someone to follow'. In the days when I write this a little episode is being shown on television as part of the propaganda to deter people from smoking. A father and son are out fishing; they sit down to eat and to rest; the father produces a cigarette and lights it; the young boy plucks a blade of grass, puts it in his mouth, and puffs at it in imitation of smoking. The father sees what is happening, and he extinguishes his cigarette, for he suddenly realises that his son will imitate him, in the wrong things as well as in the right things.

This Paul well knows. He knows what you can only call the propaganda value of a really Christian life. And so the Christian ethic, as Paul sees it, insists that the Christian must produce an example to attract and not to repel. Paul is very conscious of the Christian duty to the 'outsider', to the man outside the church. The Thessalonians are urged to live a life of honest toil 'that you may command the respect of outsiders' (1 Thessalonians 4.12). One of the qualifications of the bishop is that he must be 'well thought of by outsiders' (1 Timothy 3.7). The Colossians are urged to conduct themselves wisely towards outsiders (Colossians 4.5). Peter is equally insistent on this. He urges Christians to 'maintain good conduct among the Gentiles' so that all malicious charges and all ill-natured slanders may be seen to be demonstrably untrue (1 Peter 2.12; 3.16). Loveliest of all is Peter's advice to a Christian wife married to a heathen husband. She is to live so beautifully that her husband will be brought to Christianity without a word being spoken (1 Peter 3.1).

Greek has two words for *good*. *Agathos* simply describes a thing as being good; *kalos* describes a thing—or person—as being, not only good, but also winsome and lovely. And it is *kalos* which in the New Testament is more frequently used (cf. Matthew 5.14-16). The Christian dare not say: 'I don't care what people say or think of me.' He must care, for his life is a sermon for or against his faith.

ix. One of the most widespread demands of Paul's ethical teaching is that Christians should live at peace together. There is hardly anything about which Paul has more to say than the danger of disharmony and the necessity of harmony.

Division has always been a disease of the church. Even at the Last Supper the disciples were disputing about which of them should be greatest (Luke 22.24). The Corinthian church had its partisan support for different leaders, a situation for which the leaders themselves were in no way to blame. Paul's rebuke is that, so long as there is jealousy and strife in their society, they have no right to call themselves Christians at all (1 Corinthians 3.1-4). The Love Feast, which should have been the sign and symbol of perfect unity, has become a thing of divisions and class distinctions. And here there is something which only the newer translations reveal. In the older translations it is said that to eat and drink at the sacrament without discerning the Lord's body is the way to judgment and not to salvation. But in the best Greek text the word *Lord's* is not included. The sin is not to discern the body; that is to say, not to discern that the church is a body, not to be aware of the oneness of the church, not to be aware of the togetherness in which all its members should be joined (1 Corinthians 11.17-32). That disunity is described in verses 17-22; to it Paul describes the illness and the weakness which have fallen upon the congregation (verse 30). The danger in question is not that of not discerning that the bread and wine stand for the body of Christ; the danger is that in a church where there is no harmony and peace between Christian and Christian the sacrament of the Lord's Supper becomes a blasphemy. In Philippi there are preachers whose aim is rather to embarrass Paul than to preach Christ (Philippians 4.2). Paul fears that, when he arrives in Corinth, he may find quarrelling and jealousy (2 Corinthians 12.20). He talks about the possibility of the Galatians biting and devouring one another (Galatians 5.15). In the Pastoral Letters there is a warning to those who 'have a morbid craving for controversy', and a warning against 'wrangling among men who are depraved in mind' (1 Timothy 6.4,5).

Again and again Paul appeals for harmony. 'Live in harmony with one another,' he writes to the Romans more than once (Romans 12.16-18; 15.5,6). The Ephesians are urged to maintain the unity of the Spirit in the bond of peace (Ephesians 4.2,3). One of the greatest hymns to Christ in the New Testament is written not as theology but as an appeal to have that mind of Christ, and so to be in unity and humility of mind (Philippians 2.1-11). The hands that are lifted in prayer should be pure, without quarrelling and without anger (1 Timothy 2.8). Titus is to tell his people always to avoid quarrels and always to show courtesy (Titus 3.2).

The ethic of Paul demands that Christians should solve the problem of living together—or stop calling themselves Christians.

x. For Paul the Christian ethic is an ethic of humility. This quality of humility is stressed all over the New Testament. In the teaching of Jesus it is the proud who will be brought low and the humble who will be exalted (Matthew 23.12; Luke 14.11; 18.14). The way into the Kingdom is the way of a child's humility (Matthew 18.4). Both James and Peter quote the Old Testament saying that God gives grace to the humble and resists the proud (James 4.6,7; 1 Peter 5.5,6; Proverbs 3.34). But the great passage on humility is the passage in which Paul draws the picture of the humility of Jesus, who gave up the glory of heaven to come and to live, not only as a man, but also as a servant, and not only to live, but in the end to die, and not only to die, but to die on a cross. The perfect pattern of humility is to be found in Jesus Christ (Philippians 2.1-11). Lowliness and meekness, says the Letter to the

Ephesians, must be the hall-marks of the Christian life (Ephesians 4.2).

This was one of the new things in Christianity. It has been pointed out that in secular Greek there is no word for humility which has not got something mean and low in it. Nowhere can the difference between the Christian and the Greek ethic be seen better than in the comparison between this Christian humility and Aristotle's picture of the great-souled man, who for Aristotle is the finest character of all (Aristotle, *Nicomachean Ethics* 4.3.1-34, 1122 a 33-1125 a 17).

Aristotle's picture is as follows. The great-souled man is the man who claims much and who deserves much. The man who claims little may be modest and temperate, but he can never be great. The man who claims much without deserving it will be merely vain, not great. To be great-souled involves greatness just as to be handsome involves size. 'Small people,' says Aristotle, 'may be neat and well-made, but they cannot be handsome.' The one thing at which the great-souled man will aim is honour. It is necessary that he should be a good man. To be great-souled is the crown of the virtues, and it cannot exist without them. When persons of worth offer the great-souled man honour, he will deign to accept it; but if honour is offered to him by common people, he will utterly despise it. He will not rejoice overmuch at prosperity, and he will not grieve overmuch at adversity. He will be largely indifferent even to honour, for nothing really matters to him. This is why great-souled people usually give the impression of being haughty. The great-souled man has a contempt for others, and he is justified in despising them.

The great-souled man is fond of conferring benefits, but he dislikes receiving them, for to confer is the mark of superiority, and to receive is the mark of inferiority. If he does receive any service, he will return it with interest, for thus he will continue to be the superior party. If he gives a benefit, he will remember it; if he receives a benefit, he will prefer to forget it. He will never, or at least only with the greatest reluctance, ask for help. To those above him he will be haughty; to those beneath him he will be condescendingly gracious. The ordinary objects of ambition will have no attraction for him. He will give the impression of being idle and slow to act, for he will be interested in nothing less than great enterprises. He can never live at the will of another, for that would be slavish. He regards nothing as great; nothing to him is to be admired. He will not bear grudges, but only for the reason that he is too superior for that. He will have no interest in receiving compliments. He will like things which are beautiful and useless rather than things which are useful; he will have a slow walk, a deep voice, and a deliberate way of speaking.

Here is the picture of the conscious aristocrat, whose characteristic attitude is contempt. The Greek picture of a great man is the picture of a man who is conscious of nothing so much as of his own superiority, a man to whom a confession of need would be a confession of failure. The blessings of the Christian view are for the man conscious of his own poverty, the man sad for his own sins, the man hungry for a goodness which he is sadly conscious that he does not possess (Matthew 5.3,4,6). The Greek great man was the man who stood above and looked down. In the Christian ethic the great man is the man who looks up to God, who knows nothing so much as his own need, and who sits where his fellow men sit.

*xi.*It is basic to the ethic of Paul, as it is to the ethic of the whole New Testament, that the Christian ethic is an ethic of love. That love is not an easy-going, emotional, sentimental thing. It is not something subject to impulse and motivated by passion. It is not something which flames and then dies, at one time a burning passion, at another time almost non-existent. It is not something which depends on our likes and our dislikes for other people. It is the steady, unvarying, undefeatable determination to love men as Jesus loved them, and never, no matter what they do in response, to seek anything but their highest good. It is the goodwill that cannot be quenched. This kind of love is going to have consequences.

(a) It will dominate the attitude of the Christian towards insult and to injury. Revenge will be something which—if it enters into the picture at all—will be in the hands of God. As for us, even for the man who counts himself our enemy, there will be nothing but concern (Romans 12.19,20). The pattern of human forgiveness is the divine forgiveness. As Christ forgave us, so must we forgive others (Ephesians 4.32; Colossians 3.13). He who has been forgiven must be forgiving. This will mean that a Christian will never try to return evil for evil. He will always try to overcome evil with good (Romans 12.21; 1 Thessalonians 5.15). The Christian will practise not so much a negative policy of non-retaliation as a positive policy which by its kindness shames men into response (Romans 12.20; Proverbs 25.21,22).

(b) This Christian love will bring into personal relationships a new tolerance. Forbearance is characteristic of the Christian attitude to others (Ephesians 4.2; Philippians 4.5). Paul was well aware that different people can quite honestly hold different points of view (Romans 14.5,6). Of this tolerance two things have to be said.

First, it is the tolerance not of indifference but of love. It is tolerant not because it does not care, and not because it thinks that it does not matter, but because in sympathy it tries to understand why the other person thinks and behaves as he does. It is the tolerance which knows that there is a great deal of truth in the saying that to know all is to forgive all.

Second, a wide tolerance in non-essentials does not at all preclude the determination to take an immovable stand, when such a stand is necessary. No one would ever dare to say that Paul was a weak character. But this inflexible Paul was able to yield on matters which he regarded as non-essential or for the greater good of the community. Everyone knows what Paul thought of circumcision, yet he circumcised Timothy simply because he knew that Timothy circumcised would find opportunities for the spread of the gospel which would be closed to Timothy uncircumcised (Acts 16.3). We

know what Paul thought of the Jewish law and all its ceremonial, yet Paul was entirely willing to finance those who were
taking the Nazirite vow, when James suggested that he should
do so, as a demonstration that he was by no means a renegade
from Judaism (Acts 21.17-26). To be inflexible and to be stubborn are by no means the same thing. To be a man of principle
and to be the victim of prejudice are very different things.
Christian tolerance knows the difference between principle
and prejudice.

(c) Christian love is the control and the condition of
Christian freedom. The Christian is free, free from the
tyranny of law, free from the obligations which governed the
food and the drink of the Jew, free from a legalistic slavery.
But that freedom must never be used as an excuse for licence.
It is the freedom of a man who loves his neighbour and who
will never do anything to harm his neighbour (Galatians
5.1,13,14). It is, as Peter said, the freedom of the servant of
God (1 Peter 2.16). There is in one of the Gilbert and Sullivan
operas a song, 'Free, yet in fetters bound to my last hour'.
The Christian is free; but the Christian is bound by the fetters
of responsibility and the obligation of love.

We can see this very clearly if we set side by side two different pieces of instruction by Paul regarding food and drink. In
the Letter to the Colossians he insists that the Christian must
never be bound by the laws of the ascetic which tell him that
he must not taste this, and he must not touch that, and he
must not handle the other thing. The Christian is free to eat
and drink what he likes (Colossians 2.16,21). And yet when
he is writing to the Romans and to the Corinthians Paul issues
the warning that a man must never claim the right to eat and
to drink those things which may be the ruin of his neighbour
(Romans 14.21; 1 Corinthians 8.13). The Christian is free, but
that freedom is controlled by responsibility and conditioned
by love. Freedom without responsibility, liberty without
love are not Christian freedom and liberty, for they can do
nothing but harm.

(d) There is one other sphere in which love dominates and controls. Love must dominate the presentation and the defence of the truth. It is true that the truth must be spoken, but it must be spoken in love (Ephesians 4.15). The truth can be spoken with an almost sadistic cruelty; it can be spoken to hurt and not to cure. It is true, as the Greek philosopher said, that truth can be like the light to sore eyes, but the hurt must never be deliberate. The Christian teacher, say the Pastoral Letters, must not be quarrelsome but kindly; he must be 'an apt teacher, forbearing, correcting his opponents with gentleness' (2 Timothy 2.23-25). As Peter had it, the Christian must always be ready to defend and commend his faith, but always with gentleness and reverence (1 Peter 3.15). It is perfectly possible to win an argument and lose the person. But when the teaching and the argument are carried on in Christian love, this will not happen.

xii. There remains one last area in which the ethic of Paul has something significant to say, something which is also said in the ethic of Peter. Included in the moral literature of the ancient world there were what were called House Tables, in which the duties of the members of the family to each other were explained and codified. The New Testament has its own form of these House Tables. They deal with three relationships.

1. The relationship between husband and wife (Ephesians 5.21-33; Colossians 3.18,19; 1 Peter 3.1-7).
2. The relationship between parent and child (Ephesians 6.1-4; Colossians 3.20,21; 1 Timothy 5.4,8,16).
3. The relationship between master and servant or slave (Ephesians 6.5-9; Colossians 3.22-4.1; Philemon 16; 1 Timothy 6.1,2; 1 Peter 2.18-25).

From these passages certain things emerge.

First, in life Paul sees a natural series of subordinations—wife to husband, child to parent, servant to master. These subordinations are not in the least tyrannies or dictatorships. They are simply the inbuilt mechanism without which life cannot go on and without which it would become a chaos. Christianity is not anarchy. It is based on love; it introduces a relationship of love between people; but it sees that, unless certain leaderships are accepted, life cannot proceed. This is not feudalism, or paternalism, or the maintaining of class distinctions. A man need not always be a servant, nor for that matter need he always be a leader. But the acceptance of leadership, both in the sense of exercising it and obeying it, is part of life.

Second, Paul's ethic of personal relationship is always a reciprocal ethic. This is the other side of the subordination. Paul never lays down a right without assigning a duty to it. The duty of the leader to the subordinate is every bit as clearly stated as the duty of the subordinate to the leader. The wife must be subject to her husband, but the husband must treat her with constant kindness and courtesy and consideration (Ephesians 5.22,25,28; Colossians 3.18,19; 1 Peter 3.1,5-7). The child must obey the parent, but the parent must never by unreasonable demands drive the child to resentment or to despair (Ephesians 6.1-4; Colossians 3.20,21). The servant must give obedience and service to the master, but the master must never forget the rights of the servant (Ephesians 6.5,9; Colossians 3.22-25; 4.1; 1 Peter 2.18-25). Privilege is never all on one side. Simply to possess the leadership is to be involved in responsibility for those who are led. The ethic of Paul would bind all together in a mutual responsibility in which no man would ever make a claim on any other man without at the same time recognising his duty to that man.

Third, the whole matter is dominated by the presence of Jesus Christ and by our responsibility to God. It is to please the Lord that children must obey (Colossians 3.20). The relationship between husband and wife is like that between Christ and the church (Ephesians 5.21-33). The servant works as if he was going to take his work and offer it to Christ (Ephesians 6.6-8; Colossians 3.23,24). The master must always remember that he is not his own master, but that he has a master in heaven (Ephesians 6.9; Colossians 4.1). Earth is always related to heaven; time is always related to eternity; the simplest thing becomes a religious thing. As George Herbert had it:

> *Teach me, my God and King,*
> *   In all things thee to see;*
> *And what I do in anything,*
> *   To do it as for thee!*

> *A servant with this clause*
> *   Makes drudgery divine,*
> *Who sweeps a room as for thy laws,*
> *   Makes that and the action fine.*

Work and worship have become one and the same thing.

Fourth, the new situation had its problems. It may at first sight surprise us that in the New Testament nothing is said about emancipating the slaves. Two things are to be said. First, to have suggested the emancipation of the slaves would have produced a chaos, and in the end nothing but mass executions; and even if a move for emancipation had succeeded there was no free market for labour. The time was not ripe. Second, when Paul sent Onesimus back to Philemon, he sent him back no longer as a slave only, but also as a brother beloved (Philemon 16). This is to say that Christian love and fellowship had introduced a new relationship between master and slave in which these terms ceased to have any relevance at all. So much was this the case that in the congregation the master might well find himself receiving the sacrament from the hands of his slave. If men are together in Christian love, it does not matter if you call one servant and the other master, for they are brothers. True, the time will come when that very situation will make slavery impossible, but it had to come in its own time, or there could have been nothing but trouble.

Fifth, one last thing is to be noted. The servant is now a brother beloved; master and servant may both be Christians. There is a passage in the First Letter to Timothy which indicates that there were servants who tried to take advantage of that new relationship. 'Those who have believing masters must not be disrespectful on the ground that they are brethren; rather they must serve all the better since those who benefit by their service are believers and beloved' (1 Timothy 6.1,2). There were clearly some servants who used the new relationship to attempt to slacken discipline and to get away with idleness and shoddy work. But the Christian ethic teaches that the relationship of brotherhood should make us better and not slacker workmen, for now we work not by compulsion but in partnership with each other.

The Pauline ethic may be nineteen hundred years old, but it is still as valid as ever, and not even yet have its implications been completely worked out.

CHAPTER FOUR

Situation Ethics

When we talk about ethics, we mostly mean a series of rules and laws and principles by which we act and which tell us what to do. Mostly we take it that ethics classifies words and actions into things which are good and things which are bad, and we take it that the goodness and the badness belong to the thing as such. On the whole this is meant to simplify things and to make life easy. It means that we have got, so we think, a series of prefabricated rules and laws and principles, which we accept and apply. It saves us from the difficult and the often dangerous task of making our own judgments and deciding things for ourselves.

But in 1966 an American professor called Joseph Fletcher wrote a book called *Situation Ethics*, which has proved to be one of the most influential books written this century. Fletcher's basic principle is that there is nothing which is universally right or universally wrong; there is nothing which is intrinsically good or intrinsically bad. Goodness and badness are not built in, essential, unchangeable qualities of anything; they are only things which happen to actions in different situations; they are only descriptions of things in different circumstances; they are not properties, they are predicates. According to this theory of ethics, there is no such thing as a predefinition of goodness or badness. What we have to take to any situation is not a prefabricated decision, but an act of judgment. Throughout this chapter the arguments and the illustrations are taken mainly from Fletcher's two books, *Situation Ethics* and *Moral Responsibility*.

It has to be noted that the situation ethics man does not as it were start from nothing. He knows all the rules and the principles; he knows all that the accumulated experience of human beings has found out. He knows that there are rules and principles; but he refuses to say that any principle is absolutely binding and always valid, right or wrong in itself. Bonhoeffer said: 'Principles are only tools in the hand of God, soon to be thrown away as unserviceable.' The situationist does not deny that there are principles; he does not for a moment deny the classifications of things that experience has built up; but he completely refuses to be shackled or bound by anything.

We have got to qualify all this; for to the situationist there is one thing and one thing only that is absolutely, always and universally good—*and that one thing is love*. So Fletcher's first two propositions are:

Only one thing is intrinsically good, namely love: nothing else. The ultimate norm of Christian decisions is love: nothing else.

Quite clearly we will have to be sure of just what love is. The situationist is not talking about what we might call romantic love. In Greek there are four words for love. There is *erōs*, which means passion; there is always sex in *erōs*. There is *philia*, which is friendship-feeling; there is physical love in *philia*, but there is loyalty and companionship as well. There is *storgē*, which is love in the family circle; there is no sex in it; it is the love of a father for a daughter, a son for his mother, a brother for a sister. And there is *agapē*; this is the word. *Agapē* is unconquerable goodwill; it is the determination always to seek the other man's highest good, no matter what he does to you. Insult, injury, indifference—it does not matter; nothing but goodwill. It has been defined as purpose, not passion. It is an attitude to the other person.

This is all important, because if we talk about this kind of love, it means that we can love the person we don't like. This is not a matter of the reaction of the heart; it is an attitude of the will and the whole personality deliberately directed to the other man. You cannot order a man to fall in love in the romantic sense of the term. Falling in love is like stepping on a banana skin; it happens, and that is all there is to it. But you can say to a man: 'Your attitude to others must be such that you will never, never, never want anything but their highest good.'

Obviously, when we define love like this, love is a highly intelligent thing. We must, as the Americans say, figure the angles. We must in any situation work out what love is. What does love demand?

Suppose, for instance, a house catches fire and in it there is a baby and the original of the Mona Lisa; which do you save—the baby or the priceless and irreplaceable picture? There is really no problem here; you save the baby for a life is always of greater value than a picture.

But think of this one—suppose in the burning house there is your aged father, an old man, with the days of his usefulness at an end, and a doctor who has discovered a cure for one of the world's great killer diseases, and who still carries the formulae in his head, and you can save only one—whom do you save? Your father who is dear to you, or the doctor in whose hands there are thousands of lives? Which is love?

On the Wilderness Trail, Daniel Boone's trail westward through Cumberland Gap to Kentucky, many families in the trail caravans lost their lives to the Indians. A Scottish woman had a baby at the breast. The baby was ill and crying, and the baby's crying was betraying her other three children and the rest of the party; the party clearly could not remain hidden if the baby continued crying; their position would be given away. Well, the mother clung to the baby; the baby's cries led the Indians to the position; and the party was discovered and all were massacred. There was another such occasion. On this occasion there was a Negro woman in the party. Her baby too was crying and threatening to betray the party. She strangled the baby with her own two hands to stop its crying—and the whole party escaped. Which action was love? The action of the mother who kept her baby and brought death to it and to herself and to all, or the action of the mother who killed the baby and saved the lives of the caravan? Here is the kind of decision with which the situationist confronts us; which action was love?

The situationist is always confronting us with decisions. There is no absolute right and wrong; we have to work it out in each situation. There are principles, of course, but they can only advise; they do not have the right of veto. Any principle must be abandoned, left, disregarded, if the command to love your neighbour can be better served by so doing.

The situationist is sure that a rigid sticking to the rules is all wrong. It can produce what someone called 'the immorality of morality'. It can produce what Mark Twain called 'a good man in the worst sense of the term'. A French priest said that fanatic love of virtue has done more harm than all the vices put together. It is the situation that counts. There are times when justice can become unjust. So Fletcher tells two stories, the first from real life, the second from a play.

A friend of Fletcher's arrived in St Louis just as a presidential campaign was ending. He took a cab and the cab-driver volunteered the information: 'I and my father and my grandfathers and their fathers have always been straight ticket Republicans.' 'Ah,' said Fletcher's friend who is himself a Republican, 'I take it that means you will vote for Senator So-and-so.' 'No,' said the driver, 'there are times when a man has to push his principles aside, and do the right thing!' There are times when principles become wrong—even when they are right.

The other is a story from Nash's play *The Rainmaker*. The Rainmaker makes love to a spinster girl in a barn at midnight. He does not really love her, but he is determined to save her from becoming spinsterised; he wants to give her back her womanhood, and to rekindle her hopes of marriage and children. Her morally outraged brother threatens to shoot him. Her father, a wise old rancher, says to his son: 'Noah,

you're so full of what's right that you can't see what's good.'
For the situationist a thing that is labelled wrong can be in
certain circumstances the only right thing.

This leads us to the second of Fletcher's basic principles.
Fletcher lays it down:

Love and justice are the same thing, for justice is love distributed, nothing else.

We can relate love and justice in different ways. Sometimes
people think of love *versus* justice, as if love and justice were
against each other; or love *or* justice, as if you had to choose
one or the other, but could not have both; or love *and* justice
as if the two things complemented each other. But for
Fletcher love *is* justice; love and justice are one and the same
thing. This is a new idea. Niebuhr, the great American teacher,
used to say that the difference is that love is transcendent and
love is impossible; while justice is something by which we can
live in this present society. Brunner held that the difference is
that love must be between two persons; whereas justice exists
between groups. But Fletcher will have it that love is the same
thing as justice. How does he make this out?

Accept the fact that the one absolute is love. Then love has
to be worked out in the situations of life—and the working
of it out is justice. Justice, it is said, consists of giving each
man his due; but the one thing that is due to every man is
love; therefore love and justice are the same. Justice, says
Fletcher, is love distributed. When we are confronted with
the claims of more than one person, of three or four people,
we have to give them love, and it is justice which settles just
how love is to be applied to each of them. Justice is love
working out its problems.

So then unless love is to be a vague sentimental generalised
feeling, there must be justice, because justice is love applied
to particular cases. This is precisely what is so often the matter
with love, the fact that it never gets worked out and never
gets beyond being a feeling and an emotion. Some time ago—
Fletcher cites the case—Sammy Davis Jr. the great enter-

tainer became a Jew, and thereby repudiated Christianity. 'As I see it,' he said, 'the difference is that the Christian religion preaches, Love thy neighbour, and the Jewish religion preaches justice, and I think that justice is the big thing we need.' Sammy Davis is black, and he knew all about so-called Christian love. As Fletcher says, there are many people who would claim that they love black people, and who at the same time deny them simple justice. Fletcher goes on: 'To paraphrase the classic cry of protest, we can say: To hell with your love; we want justice.' This is exactly what happens when justice and love are not equated.

This means that love has always got to be thinking; love has always got to be calculating. Otherwise love is like the bride who wanted to ignore all recipes and simply let her love for her husband guide her when she was baking him a cake. Love has to think, wisely, deeply, intelligently. Fletcher goes on to illustrate the kind of problem love must face and solve.

Take the case of a nurse in a TV play called *The Bitter Choice*. She was in charge of a ward in a military hospital for wounded soldiers, and she acted with deliberate and calculated severity and even harshness to make the wounded soldiers hate her so much that the one thing they wanted was to get on their feet again and get out. Was this cruelty or was it a far more real love than the love which coddled and comforted until the men had no wish to leave the hospital at all?

Take the case of a doctor. A doctor is bound not to divulge any of the affairs of his patients. In his Hippocratic oath he promises:

> Whatever in my professional practice—or even not in connection with it—I see or hear in the lives of men which ought not to be spoken of abroad, I will not divulge, deeming that on such matters we should be silent.

The doctor knows that a marriage is going to take place. He knows both parties; he knows that the girl is a virgin and is pure; he happens to know that the boy has been a libertine and has syphilis. What is the duty of love? Does the doctor keep

74

his oath? If a doctor began to talk it would create a situation that would be intolerable. Or does he tell the girl? Which is love?

Suppose in a public works a personnel manager has on his staff a clerk in bad health and rendered inefficient through illness, where does *agapē*, love, concern lie? Does he keep the clerk on? Or does he think of the workers on the production-line whose output and piece rate are being cut by the inevitable delays caused by this clerk's inefficiency due to his health condition? Which is love? Which is the Christian thing to do?

In one of Sinclair Lewis's novels there is a scientist Dr Arrowsmith. He has discovered a serum which he knows to be a certain cure for a plague that regularly attacks a Caribbean island. He cannot persuade the government and the authorities to accept his claim. Plague hits the island. Arrowsmith inoculates half the inhabitants; and deliberately refuses to inoculate the other half. He knows that those inoculated will recover and he knows that those not inoculated will die. He deliberately sacrifices them to convince the government of the effectiveness of his serum, and thus to save thousands of lives in the future. Is this love? Is this the real concern?

Fletcher quotes a war incident which happened in Italy. A priest in the underground movement bombed and destroyed a Nazi freight train. The occupying Germans then began killing twenty prisoners a day, and said that they would go on doing so until the saboteur was handed over or surrendered. The priest refused to give himself up, not because he contemplated more sabotage, but because, so he said, there was no other priest available in the district, and the people needed the absolution he could give for their souls' sake. After three days a fellow resistance fighter deliberately betrayed the priest in order to stop the massacre of prisoners. Was he right? Was what looked like an act of treachery in fact an act of love?

Love has got to calculate. And it may well be that love has

to use methods which in other circumstances would be terrible things. The argument of the situationist is that nothing is absolutely good or bad; it all depends on the situation and in certain situations even an act of treachery may be an act of love.

Let us return to the ten commandments. The situationist knows the ten commandments; he respects them; he does not merely toss them aside; but he is prepared to say that there can come times when any of the ten commandments may become a bad thing and when it may be a Christian duty to break any or all of them.

Let us look at some of the examples that Fletcher produces. What about the commandment: You must not steal?

If a homicidal maniac had possession of a gun, surely it would be a duty and not a sin to steal it from him. Suppose a man was hellbent on murder, and he was mad. Suppose he came up to you and asked you where his intended victim was, and suppose you knew, surely it would be a duty to mislead the man rather than to give him the information you were asked for; surely a lie in this case is the right thing. Oddly enough, some ethical teachers do not think so. They think that you ought to tell the man the truth. They argue that if you do that, there will only be one sin—murder; whereas if you tell a lie and then afterwards the murderer does in spite of your lie get his victim, there will be two sins, lying and murder.

What about the commandment that you must not kill? When T. E. Lawrence was leading his Arabs two of his men had a quarrel and in the quarrel Hamed killed Salem. Lawrence knew that Salem's people would be out for vengeance, and he knew that a blood feud would arise in which both families would be involved, and that one whole family would be out to murder the other whole family. What did Lawrence do? He thought it out and then with his own hands he killed Hamed and thus stopped the blood feud. Was this right? Was this action which stopped a blood feud and probably prevented scores of people from being murdered an act of murder or an act of love?

Take the case of the commandment which forbids adultery. Here Fletcher cites two illustrations, both from films. The first is from the film *Never on Sunday*. The film was originally cited by H. A. Williams in the volume entitled *Soundings*. The point he was making was that the biggest thing in life is generous self-giving, giving as God gives. And he was saying that a good deal of what we call Christian virtue is based on fear and on the refusal totally to give oneself to another. He applies this to sexual relationships. Sexual relationships are always wrong when they merely exploit the other person. But even in relationships outside marriage there can be this total self-giving. So he tells the story of the film, a Greek film. A prostitute in the Piraeus is picked up by a young sailor. When he gets to her room he is nervous and very ill at ease. She soon sees that he is not troubled by any idea of doing wrong, but that he doubts his own virility and his capacity for physical union at all. He is a prey to destructive doubt, not to moral scruples. She gives herself to him in such a way that he acquires confidence and self-respect. I quote Williams: 'He goes away a deeper, fuller person than he came in. What is seen in this is an act of charity which proclaims the glory of God. The man is equipped for life as he never was before.' Fornication or the wonderful cure of the personality of a psychologically maladjusted man; the transgression of God's law or the fulfilment of God's will; sin or love—which?

The second illustration is from an English film called *The Mark*. In it there is a man whose abnormality is that he is a danger to small girls. The abnormality springs from the fact that he is really afraid to commit himself to an adult woman. Time goes on and he meets a woman who inspires him with enough confidence to go away with her for a weekend. They occupy separate rooms at the hotel; but it is clear that until he summons up enough confidence to sleep with her he will never be delivered from that dreadful abnormality which is on the way to destroying himself and others. In the end—I quote—they sleep together and he is made whole. Williams goes on to say: 'Where there is healing, there is Christ, whatever the church says about fornication, and the appropriate response is: Glory to God in the Highest.' Is it God or the devil? Is it love or lust? Is it sin or love? Which? (It has been pointed out to me by experts in this field that in any event such action would by no means necessarily result in a cure.)

Are we going to be driven to this conclusion that nothing is absolutely right and that apparently still less is anything absolutely wrong, and that it all depends on the situation? Is it true that goodness and badness are not qualities which are built into actions, but things which happen to an action within a situation, that they are not properties but predicates?

Let us take one last example from Fletcher. He entitles it Sacrificial Adultery. As the Russian armies drove forward to meet the Americans and the British, a Mrs Bergmeier, who was out foraging for food for her children and herself, was picked up. Without being able to get a word to the children she was taken away to a prison work camp in the Ukraine. Meanwhile her husband was captured and ended up in a prison camp in Wales. Ultimately the husband was released. He came back to Germany and after weeks of search he found the children, the two youngest in a Russian detention school and the oldest hiding in a cellar. They had no idea where their mother was. They never stopped searching for her. They knew that only her return could ever knit that family together again after all that had happened to them. Meanwhile away in the Ukraine a kindly camp commandant told Mrs Bergmeier that her family were together again and that they were trying to find her. But he could not release her, for release was only given for two reasons. First, a prisoner was released if he or she was suffering from a disease with which the camp could not cope, and was in that case moved to a Russian hospital. Second, a woman was released if she became pregnant. In that case women were returned to Germany as being a liability and no use for work. Mrs Bergmeier thought it out, and finally she decided to ask a friendly Volga German camp guard to make her pregnant. He did. Her condition was medically verified. She was sent back to Germany and received with open arms by her family. She told them what she had done and they thoroughly approved. In due time the baby was born. Dietrich they called him and they loved him most of all because they felt he had done more for them than any one of the others. And for the German guard they had nothing but a grateful and affectionate memory. So what? Right or wrong? Adultery or love? Which?

Fletcher holds that, when an act of intercourse has no love in it, inside or outside marriage, it is wrong. When it has no care, no concern, no love, no commitment, nothing but the satisfaction of desire—in or outside marriage—it is wrong. Fletcher quotes a cartoon from one of the glossy magazines of sex. A dishevelled young male is holding a dishevelled young female in his arms, emerging from the blankets and saying: 'Why talk of love at a time like this?' It is better—so Fletcher says—to live together unmarried in commitment and loyalty and responsibility than to live in marriage with no love.

What, then, are we to say to all this? The situationist claims that nothing is absolutely right and nothing is absolutely wrong; it all depends on the situation. Goodness and badness are not something intrinsic, but things that happen to actions in the doing. What are we to say?

First, we can begin with something which is a criticism not so much of situation ethics as it is of Fletcher's presentation of it. The trouble is that by far the greater number of Fletcher's illustrations are drawn from the abnormal, the unusual and the extraordinary. I am not very likely to be confronted with an Arab blood feud or a war situation in Eastern Germany. It is much easier to agree that extraordinary situations need extraordinary measures than to think that there are no laws for ordinary everyday life.

Second—and this is a much more serious matter—situation ethics presents us with a terrifying degree of freedom. There we are in front of our situation; we have no prefabricated judgment; *you*—just *you*—have to make the right decision. Brunner has said that there is nowhere you can go—not even to the Sermon on the Mount and say: 'Now I know what to do.' There is no such thing as a readymade decision. Of course, we know the things that experience has discovered and teaches, but we are left alone in complete freedom to apply them.

Fletcher is quite right when he says that basically men do not want freedom. He quotes the legend of the Grand Inquisitor in Dostoievsky's book, *The Brothers Karamazov*, which is a parable of the terrible burden of freedom. Jesus returns to this earth. The Inquisitor recognises him in the crowd, watching a religious procession, and immediately has him arrested. In the dead of night the Inquisitor secretly goes to Jesus. He tries to explain to Jesus that people do not want freedom. They want security. If you really love people, he argues, you want to make them happy, not free. Freedom is danger, openness. They want law, not responsibility; they want the neurotic comfort of rules, not the spiritual open places of decision-making. Christ, he says, must not start again all that old business about freedom and grace and commitment and responsibility. Let things be; let the church with its laws handle them. Will Jesus please go away.

There is no doubt that most people do not want to be continually confronted with the necessity of making decisions. They would rather have their decisions made for them; they would rather apply laws and principles to the situation. And it may well be that people are right.

The right use of freedom in our relationships with others depends on love. If love is perfect, then freedom is a good thing. But if there is no love, or if there is not enough love, then freedom can become licence, freedom can become selfishness and even cruelty. If you leave a man without love to do as he likes, then the damage that he can do is incalculable. It may well be that neither I nor any other person is at this stage ready for this lonely freedom which the situationist offers us. The situationists have a kind of phobia of law, but the lesson of experience is that we need a certain amount of law, being the kind of people we are.

Aristotle had his doctrine of habituation. He argued that there is a time when it is not possible to give a child freedom. It is not that the child is bad. It is that at the stage of childhood the child has not the wisdom or the experience, the ability to take the long view and to calculate consequences, which freedom demands. We have, therefore, at this stage to submit the child to discipline, to law, to control, so that the child develops the habit of doing the right thing. You only learn to play the flute by practising playing the flute according to the laws of flute-playing. You only learn to be good by practising goodness under the discipline—and sometimes even the punishment—of the laws of goodness. There is a stage at which the child has to be habituated and even compelled into goodness. Only after he has reached the stage of habituation is it possible to trust him with freedom.

Take the case of a game. A game would become a chaos if there were no rules. It may be that in some future sporting Utopia it will be possible for Celtic to play Rangers, or for Arsenal to play Manchester United, without a referee, but that stage has not yet come! The reign of law is still needed.

If all men were saints, then situation ethics would be the perfect ethics. John A. T. Robinson has called situation ethics 'the only ethic for man come of age'. This is probably true— but man has not yet come of age. Man, therefore, still needs the crutch and the protection of law. If we insist that in every situation every man must make his own decision, then first of all we must make man morally and lovingly fit to take that decision; otherwise we need the compulsion of law to make him do it. And the fact is that few of us have reached that stage; we still need law, we still need to be told what to do, and sometimes even to be compelled to do it.

Thirdly, the situationist points out again and again that in his view there is nothing which is intrinsically good or bad. Goodness and badness, as he puts it, are not properties, they are predicates. They are not inbuilt qualities; they happen to a thing in a given situation. I am very doubtful if the distinction between goodness and badness can be so disposed of.

We may grant that Fletcher has shown that there can be situations in which a thing generally regarded as wrong could be the right thing to do. But that does not prove that it is good. There is a close analogy here with dangerous drugs which a doctor may have to prescribe. When he describes these drugs, he does not pretend that they are not poisons. Poisons they are and poisons they remain. They have to be kept in a special cupboard and in a special container. They can only be used under the strictest safeguards. There are indeed occasions when the doctor will not prescribe them at all, because he is not certain that the patient has the strength of mind not to misuse them. These things have a kind of inbuilt red light, and that red light is not taken away, for the dangerous drug is never called anything else but a poison. So there are certain things, which on rare occasions may be used to serve a good end. But the red light should not be removed by calling them good things. They remain highly dangerous, and they should never be called, or regarded as, anything else.

I should personally go further. I think that there are things which can in no circumstances be right. To take but two examples, to start a young person in the name of experience on the experiments which can lead to drug addiction can never be right. To break up a family relationship in the name of so-called love can never be right. The right and the wrong are not so easily eliminated.

Fourth, the situationist is liable to forget two things.

(a) He is liable to forget what psychological aids can do for abnormal conditions. Fletcher took instances of cures being effected by what the Christian would simply regard as committing adultery. He cites the instance of the man who was a danger to small girls being cured by intercourse with a mature woman. It is to be noted that such an action would by no means guarantee a cure for a man in such a condition anyway. He quotes the play *The Rainmaker*, in which the Rainmaker deliberately seduces the farmer's daughter to save her, as he claimed, from being 'spinsterised'. This completely leaves out of account the very real possibility of sublimation. 'Sublimation', Dr Hadfield says, 'is the process by which instinctive emotions are diverted from their original ends and redirected to purposes satisfying the individual and of value to the community.' There is no need for repression with all its attendant evils. It is a perfectly normal thing for the force and the power and the surge that can flow through one instinct to be sublimated in the service of another. A man or a woman may have no outlet for the instinct of sex, and time and again that force of sex can be canalised into other channels and sublimated in the service of other things. There is many an unmarried woman who is very, very far from being a 'frustrated spinster' because she has found fullness of life in some other outlet. There is many a man who has had to do without marriage and who has sublimated his sex drive into other achievements and other service. One may speculate whether John Wesley would have been such a dynamic founder of a new church if he had been happily married. He poured into the church what he might have kept within the limits of a home. There are cures and compensations for abnormal conditions which do not involve breaking what we have learned to call the moral law—and in point of fact these cures are far more effective.

(b) And above all, the situationist is liable to forget quite simply the grace of God. Unless Christianity is a total swindle, then it must make good its claim to make bad men good. To encourage towards permissiveness is no real cure; to direct to the grace of God is. When John Wesley entered on open-air preaching, and when he saw what the grace of God could do, he wrote to his brother Samuel:

> I will show you him who was a lion till then, and is now a lamb; him that was a drunkard, and is now exemplarily sober; the whoremonger that was, who now abhors the very garment spotted with the flesh.

These, said Wesley, are the arguments for, and the proofs of, the power of the grace of God—and that power is still as strong as ever.

The situationists have taught us that we must indeed be flexible; that we must indeed look on the problems of others, not with self-righteousness, but with sympathy; that we must not be legalists; but in spite of that we do well still to remember that there are laws which we break at our peril.

In the background of our discussion of situation ethics there has always been the idea of *law*. Sometimes, in fact, it has almost seemed that the idea of law and the idea of situation ethics formed a contrast and even an antithesis. I did say at one point that the situationists seemed to have a phobia of law. Before we leave this subject, it will therefore be well to look at the conception of law in general, so that, if we do discard law, we may see what we are discarding. What then is law, and what does law do, or what is law intended to do, for society?

i. It may be said to begin with that law is the distillation of experience. Law seeks to ensure that those courses of action which experience has shown to be beneficial are followed, and to eliminate those courses of action which experience has proved to be harmful and injurious to society and its members. Law is thus a summary of society's experience of life and living. Therefore, to discard law is to discard experience. This is not by any means a full description of law, for it will clearly make a very great difference which courses of action any particular society has decided to be good or bad.

ii. This may be put in another way. It has been said that 'law is the rule of reason applied to existing circumstances'.

Fletcher has said that law is that which seeks to ensure that people will live life as a reasonable man would live it. Again, it has been said that 'law translates morals (value judgments) into social disciplines' (J. Fletcher, *Moral Responsibility*, p. 94). A society comes to a conclusion what a reasonable life is. It comes to a conclusion as to what it will take as its working values and as to what is dangerous to these values. It then frames a code of laws the intention of which is to ensure that this approved way of life and these chosen values can be followed.

iii. One of the main functions of law is definition. It defines what is to be punished and what is to be approved. It defines what is a crime and it lays down the point at which restraint will be exercised on the man who refuses to conform. There is a sense in which law not only defines but creates a crime. For instance, for long polygamy was perfectly legal as, for example, in patriarchal times in the Old Testament; then monogamy becomes the law, and that which was once legal becomes a crime. It is law's function to define that which at any time society forbids.

iv. Law has, or at least can have, two opposite effects. First, by defining the wrong things the law intends to dissuade people from doing them. It may either dissuade by making people afraid of the consequences of doing the wrong thing, or by creating in them a sense of responsibility for maintaining the society of which they are a part.

But, second, law can have an unfortunate effect. The very forbidding of a thing can create a desire for that thing, as Paul so vividly shows in Romans 7: 'If it had not been for the law, I should not have known sin. I should not have known what it is to covet, if the law had not said, "You shall not covet".' The thing is no sooner forbidden than it becomes attractive. This was what the boy Augustine discovered about the stolen pears:

There was a pear tree near our vineyard, laden with fruit. One stormy night we rascally youths set out to rob it and carry our spoils away. We took off a huge load of pears—not to feast upon ourselves, but to throw them to the pigs, though we ate just enough to have the pleasure of forbidden fruit. They were nice pears, but it was not the pears that my wretched soul coveted, for I had plenty better at home. I picked them simply in order to become a thief. The only feast I got was a feast of iniquity, and that I enjoyed to the full. What was it that I loved in that theft? Was it the pleasure of acting against the law, in order that I, a prisoner under rules, might have a maimed counterfeit of freedom by doing what was forbidden? . . . The desire to steal was awakened simply by the prohibition of stealing.

The sweetness of the pears lay in the fact that they were stolen pears. In the days before consenting homosexuality was legalised, Westermarck quoted a homosexual as saying that 'he would be very sorry to see the English law changed, as the practice would then lose its charm' (E. Westermarck, *Christianity and Morals*, p. 374; qtd. J. Fletcher, *Moral Responsibility*, p. 103).

Law is a double-edged force. Its prohibitions may dissuade, but they may encourage.

v. Law is for the protection of society. Law is meant for the control of the man who would injure society. Law is ordinary people uniting and banding themselves together to control the strong, bad man. A number of small boys may make common cause against the bully, against whom singly they would be helpless; so they combine to control him. So law is a defensive and protective alliance by the mass of ordinary people to control and restrain the man who for his own ends would injure or exploit or dominate society. Law exists for the protection of the ordinary citizen.

vi. I have left to the end one very important view of law. It is a view which is largely, but not quite universally, accepted. It is the view that it is always public morals with which the law is concerned, and never private morals, unless these private morals are an offence to public decency or a threat to public welfare. In other words, there are many things which are immoral, but which are not illegal. Or, to put it in another way, there is a wide difference between *sin*, with which the law is not concerned, and *crime*, with which the law is deeply concerned. To take the case of sexual morality, so long as a sexual act is by common consent between two adults, so long as it cannot be held to have hurt or injured either, and so long as it is carried on in a way that does not offend public decency or interfere with public order, then it is not the concern of the law. This has always been the law in regard to prostitution in this country. It has never been illegal to have sexual intercourse with a prostitute. What is illegal is solicitation, which is an offence against public order. Very recently, the situation has become the same in regard to homosexual practices, which until then were illegal as such.

This point of view is stated in the words of the Church of England Moral Welfare Council:

It is not the function of the State and the law to constitute themselves guardians of private morality, and thus to deal with sin as such belongs to the province of the church. On the other hand, it is the duty of the State to punish crimes, and it may properly take cognizance of, and define as criminal, those sins which also constitute offences against public morality.

Similarly, the Wolfenden Report says:

It should not be the duty of the law to concern itself with immorality as such . . . It should confine itself to these activities which offend against public order and decency, or expose the ordinary citizens to what is offensive and injurious.

On this view the law has nothing to do with a man's private morals, but everything to do with his public conduct. It is not only what we might call public pronouncements which take this point of view. There is a letter from C. S. Lewis to Mrs Edward A. Allen, written in 1958, which takes exactly the same view:

I quite agree with the Archbishop that no *sin*, simply as such, should be made a *crime*. Who the deuce are our rulers to enforce their opinions about sin on us?—a lot of professional politicians, often venal time-servers, whose opinion on a moral problem in one's own life we should attach very little value to. Of course, many acts which are sins against God are also injuries to our fellow-citizens, and must on that account, but only on that account, be made crimes. But of all the sins in the world I should have thought that homosexuality was the one that least concerns the State. We hear too much of the State. Government is at its best a necessary evil. Let's keep it in its place (*Letters of C. S. Lewis*, ed. W. H. Lewis, p. 281).

So the official and the personal point of view combine to hold that private morality is no affair of the State or of the law, unless it has public effects. For the moment we shall leave this, and we shall very soon return to it.

The trouble about this whole question is that it presents us with a series of tensions, which are built into the problem of the connection between morality and law.

i. There is the tension between freedom and law. Here the situationists are very definite. Fletcher writes: 'Nothing we do is truly moral unless we are free to do otherwise. We must be free to decide what to do before any of our actions even begin to be moral. No discipline but self-discipline has any moral significance. This applies to sex, politics or anything else. A moral act is a free act, done because we want to . . . Morality is meaningless apart from freedom' (J. Fletcher, *Moral Responsibility*, p. 136).

On the face of it, this is true. But—and it is a very big but—who of us is, in fact, free? Our heredity, our environment, our upbringing, the traditions we have inherited, our temperament, the cumulative effect of our previous decisions all have an effect upon us. Again it is of the first importance that freedom does not only mean that a man is free to do a thing; it must also mean that he is free *not* to do it—and that is exactly where our past comes in. Most of us have made ourselves such that we are not free. The whole trouble about freedom is that for many of us it is an illusion.

If a man was really free, then we might agree that he must be given an unrestricted choice; but in the human situation, as it is, man, as he is, cannot do without law to persuade and even to compel him to do what is right. This is not to plead for a régime of law and it is not to reject a régime of freedom, for here we are certainly confronted not with an either/or but with a both/and. Freedom and law go hand in hand, and it may be the truest proposition of all that it is by the influence of law that people come in the end to be really free. And, to be fair, this is precisely where Fletcher comes down, for in the end he writes: 'In the language of classical biblical theology in the West, grace reinforces law and sometimes even bypasses it, but it does not abolish it, nor can it replace it, until sin itself is no more' (J. Fletcher, *Moral Responsibility*, p. 94).

ii. There is the tension between immorality and illegality. We have already made the point that there are many things which are immoral but which are not illegal. For instance, to take a crude example, prostitution is immoral, but it is not illegal. We have seen that the common, one might say the orthodox, view is that the law has nothing to do with private morals, but only with public morality. Not everyone agrees with that. So prominent a jurist as Lord Devlin did not agree with the Wolfenden Report. He said that it was wrong to talk of 'private morality' at all. He holds that 'the suppression of vice is as much the law's business as the suppression of subversive activities'. There is no doubt that this is a very difficult doctrine, if for no other reason than that it would be hard to get people to agree as to what vice in fact is. Fletcher quotes a section from the Sycamore Report from America: 'Let Christians face squarely the fact that what the body of authoritative Christian thought passed off as God's revealed truth was in fact human error with a Pauline flavour. Let us remember this fact every time we hear a solemn assertion about this or that being God's will or the Christian ethic.' The difficulty would be to define vice.

But suppose we do accept the Christian ethic as it is in the teaching of Jesus; suppose we accept it ourselves and suppose that we are convinced that it is the best prescription for the life of society. Are we then quite happy if the law progressively makes what we think wrong easier? Are we quite happy about the legalising of consenting homosexuality? Are we quite happy about the easing of divorce regulations? Would we be quite happy to find it enacted that unmarried students living together and begetting a child should then become eligible for the same grants as married people? The trouble is that once a thing is not forbidden, it may be felt not only to be permitted but to be encouraged. It could be argued that what the law permits, it approves. Take the case of the university-student relationship. No longer is the university *in loco parentis*, in the place of the parent; paternalism is out. But take especially the case of the residential universities. It is argued that in his rooms the student has the right to do as he likes, to live his own life, and that the university has no right to interfere with his 'private' life. But what if he makes his rooms a centre of what some people would still call seduction? What if he does have a girl in bed with him all night? What if he does make his rooms a centre for experiment in the taking of drugs? Is the university in such a case to be strictly neutral? Must the university stand by and see at least some students emerge from its life intellectually wiser and morally worse? Of course, if we say we no longer accept any Christian standards, then the question does not arise. But this we have not yet said, and so long as these standards are accepted, then sheer and absolute permissiveness is not possible. It is here, in fact, that the public aspect of private morality comes in. A man can live his own life, but when he begins deliberately to alter the lives of others, then a real problem arises, on which we cannot simply turn our backs, and in which there is a place for law as the encourager of morality.

iii. There is the tension between the individual and the community. This is the tension between individualism and solidarity. In the early days of Judaism there was such solidarity that the individual as an individual had hardly any independent existence. When Achan's sin was discovered his whole family was stoned along with him (Joshua 7). They say that to this day if you ask a man in a primitive society what his name is, he will begin by telling you, not his name, but his tribe. But in our time it is the individual who is stressed. Self-development, self-expression, self-realisation have become the watchwords of modern society. Too much law means the obliteration of the individual; too much individualism means the weakening of law. It so happens that today we are living in a time of individualism, but a man will do well to remember that it can never be right to develop himself at the expense of others.

We may well come to the conclusion that one of the great problems of the present situation is to adjust the delicate balance between freedom and law, and between the individual and society. And the only solution is that a man should discover what it means to love his neighbour as himself.

CHAPTER FIVE

The Teaching of the New Testament about Work

Work—a curse or a blessing—which is it? Here are two poems with precisely opposite ideas of work. The first is four lines of doggerel which were written by a charwoman who was very tired and who was dying:

> *Don't pity me now;*
> *Don't pity me never;*
> *I'm going to do nothing*
> *For ever and ever.*

The one thing in the world she wanted was to be done for ever with work. Dr Johnson, who was nothing if not honest, once said: 'We would all be idle if we could.'

But here is Rudyard Kipling's dream of what he wanted when life had ended:

> *When earth's last picture is painted,*
> *and the tubes are twisted and dried,*
> *When the oldest colours are faded,*
> *and the youngest critic has died,*
> *We shall rest and faith we shall need it—*
> *lie down for an aeon or two*
> *Till the Master of all Good Workmen*
> *shall put us to work anew.*

> *And those that were good shall be happy:*
> *they shall sit in a golden chair;*
> *They shall splash at a ten-league canvas*
> *with brushes of comets' hair.*

> *They shall find real saints to draw from,*
>   *Magdalene, Peter and Paul,*
> *They shall work for an age at a sitting,*
>   *and never grow tired at all.*

> *And only The Master shall praise us,*
>   *and only The Master shall blame;*
> *And no one shall work for money,*
>   *and no one shall work for fame,*
> *But each for the joy of the working,*
>   *and each in his separate star,*
> *Shall draw the Thing as he sees It*
>   *for the God of Things as They are.*

Here are two opposite points of view. In the one case the end of life is the end of work—and thank God! In the other case the end of life is the opportunity to work as never before—and praise God! It so happens that these two points of view can both be found in the Bible, though not with equal emphasis. The conclusion of the old Genesis story is that Adam and Eve are for ever shut out of the garden, and the condemnation is: 'In the sweat of your face you shall eat bread' (Genesis 3.17-19). The idea is that, if man had not sinned, he would have lived for ever in the sun-kissed paradise with nothing to do but to enjoy the garden.

On the other hand, almost the whole Bible, apart from this story, bases its entire thought on the teaching and the assumption that man is meant to work and to work honourably and well. 'There is nothing better,' said the preacher, 'than that a man should enjoy his work' (Ecclesiastes 3.22). In the teaching of Jesus parable after parable is based on the fact that a good servant must be a good workman.

Paul was quite clear that if a man refused to work, he had no right to eat (2 Thessalonians 3.10), and it is his own claim and his boast that he supported himself with his own two hands, and took nothing for nothing from anyone (1 Thessalonians 2.9; 2 Thessalonians 3.8). And there is the astonishing case of Jesus. Jesus was no less than thirty years of age when he emerged into public life (Luke 3.23). It was as the carpenter of Nazareth that people knew him (Mark 6.2). For thirty of his thirty-three years on earth he was a village workman. There is a legend that he made the best ox-yokes in Galilee and that men beat a track to his shop to buy them. In those days they had signs over their shops as they have now, and it has been suggested that the sign on Jesus' shop door was an ox-yoke and the writing: 'My yokes fit well.' 'My yoke is easy' (Matthew 11.30)—not in the sense that it is no bother, but in the sense that shoes are easy, that they fit well. It is quite certain that, if Jesus had not done the work of the shop in Nazareth well, he would never have been given by God the work of saving the world. Jesus began by being a working man.

This was one of the basic differences between the Jewish and the Greek and Roman world. To a Jew work was essential; work was of the essence of life. The Jews had a saying that he who does not teach his son a trade teaches him to steal. A Jewish rabbi was the equivalent of a college lecturer or professor, but according to the Jewish law he must take not a penny for teaching; he must have a trade at which he worked with his hands and by which he supported himself. So there were rabbis who were tailors and shoemakers and barbers and bakers and even perfumers. Work to a Jew was life.

But the Greek and Roman civilisations were based on slavery. According to Plato, no artisan could be a citizen of the ideal state. Aristotle tells us that in Thebes no man could become a citizen until ten years after he had stopped working at a trade. Cicero lays it down that no gentleman will work for a wage; no gentleman will buy or sell either wholesale or retail. 'No workshop can have any culture about it.'

Unquestionably the Christian tradition came from the Jewish tradition. Work for the Jew and for the Christian is the making of life. Work and life are the same thing. We can begin by saying certain quite general things about work.

The Teaching of New Testament about Work

i. First, our work is what we are and where we are. There is nothing commoner than for a person to wish that his work was other than that it is. The worker in industry or in a factory might wish to be a minister or a doctor, and there are times when the minister and the doctor covet enviously a job that begins at 9 a.m. and finishes at 5.30 p.m. instead of a job that goes on for twenty-four hours a day. Carlyle was one of Scotland's great thinkers and writers; his father was a stone-mason and a famous builder of bridges; and Thomas Carlyle used to say that he would rather have built one of his father's bridges than written all his own books.

There was a famous Jewish rabbi called Zusya. Sometimes he used to wish that he was other than he was. And then he said very wisely: 'In the world to come they will not ask me, Why were you not Moses? They will ask, Why were you not Zusya?' A man's duty is literally to be himself.

Rita Snowden quotes a poem in one of her books; she says that it was written by a girl of nineteen years of age, but she does not name the author:

> *Lord of all pots and pans and things*
> *Since I've no time to be*
> *A saint by doing lovely things*
> *Or watching late with thee,*
> *Or dreaming in the dawnlight,*
> *Or storming heaven's gates,*
> *Make me a saint by getting meals*
> *And washing up the plates.*
>
> *Thou who didst love to give men food*
> *In room or by the sea,*
> *Accept this service that I do—*
> *I do it unto thee.*

So then our work is first and foremost what we are and where we are. This is not to say that no man ought to change his job, or want another job; but it is to say that the best way to a

95

greater job is to do the one we have supremely well. It is the strange paradox that the man who gets the greater job is the man who is so intensely interested in what he is doing that he does not think of any other job.

ii. The New Testament is quite sure that there is no better test of a man than the way in which he works. Again and again this is the keypoint of the parables of Jesus. All that a man has to show God is his work—and that does not mean *what* he has done so much as *how* he did it.

L. P. Jacks used to tell of an old Irish navvy who worked on the construction of railways long before the days of mechanical shovels and bulldozers and excavators, in the days when all they had was a shovel and a barrow. The old navvy's spade was so well used that it shone like stainless steel when he cleaned the mud off it at night. Some one once asked him jestingly: 'Well, Paddy, what will you do when you die and when God asks you what you have to say for yourself?' 'I think', said Paddy, 'that I'll just show him my spade.' L. P. Jacks was the author of many books, and he wrote his manuscripts by hand. When he wrote he always wore an old tweed jacket, and the right cuff of the jacket was worn away with rubbing against the desk as he wrote. 'If it comes to that,' Jacks used to say, 'I think I'll show God the cuff of my jacket.'

Work is the test—not the importance of the work from the prestige point of view, but the fidelity with which it is done. It has been truly said that God does not so much need people to do extraordinary things as he needs people who do ordinary things extraordinarily well.

iii. The test of a man is work; and we can put that in another way—the test of a workman is, Does he earn his pay? Or, to put it better, does he try to earn his pay? We have in these days come perilously near to a situation in which a man is thinking, not of earning his pay, but of getting more and more pay for less and less work. If this was an ideal world, we would all be more interested in the quality of the work we produced than in the pay we got for it. It is hardly possible to rise to that height, except for the creative artist whose work is a thing of the spirit. But we are at a stage just now when the right to be paid is demanded, when the right to bargain for more is demanded, when the right to take action for the highest possible pay is demanded, and when the obligation to earn that pay is seldom admitted. Rudyard Kipling, a long time ago now, wrote a poem with this verse in it:

> *From forge and farm and mine and bench,*
> *Deck, altar, outpost lone,*
> *Mill, school, battalion, counter, trench,*
> *Rail, senate, sheepfold, throne,*
> *Creation's cry goes up on high*
> *From age to cheated age:*
> *'Send us the men who do the work*
> *For which they draw the wage.'*

iv. There is one thing which would go far to make work what it ought to be, and to cause it to be done in the spirit in which it ought to be done; and that is, if we could look at our work as a contribution owed to the community.

One of the most famous of all economic principles is the principle associated with the name of Adam Smith—the principle of the division of labour. By that principle no one tries to do everything, but each person does his own job. The baker does not try to make clothes and the tailor does not try to bake bread. The shoemaker does not try to fillet fish and the fishmonger does not try to sole shoes. Each man does his part and the whole makes up an efficient society. It is a case of each for all and all for each. This is not only good economics; it is also good Christianity. For this is the principle of the community as a body in which each part has its own part to play.

But the trouble today is that there is little or no community in life. Each section of the community is out to further its own interests, often regardless of the interest of the other parts of

97

the community, and, it would seem, always regardless of the interest of the community as a whole. If men and women worked to contribute to the community instead of to extract from the community, the community would be in a much more healthy state than it is today.

It is easy—and it is unfair—to point out all the faults and to give the impression that the duty is all on one side. Just as a man has obligations which he must satisfy and responsibilities which he must fulfil, he has certain things which are due to him; and, if these things are not given to him, there is bound to be trouble—and that trouble extends far beyond its own generation, for there is such a thing as racial memory. We see racial memory at work in animals. For instance, a dog will turn round and round before he lies down to sleep, because at one time his ancestors lay down in the long grass and they had to make a comfortable hollow before they slept. So in society today we get discontents and fears and resentments which are not the result of present conditions at all, but which are the result of injustices and inhumanities which happened two or three generations ago. The trouble in society is that if we sow the wind we reap the whirlwind. It often happens that men are fighting again—quite unconsciously—the battles their fathers and their grandfathers fought—and in the present conditions quite unnecessarily. So, then, just as there are certain things due *from* a man there are also certain things due *to* a man.

The teaching of Jesus has certain implications; they are specially prominent in the Parable of the Labourers in the Vineyard (Matthew 20.1-16).

i. There is first of all *the right of a man to work*. It is astonishing how recently the working man acquired any rights at all. As late as the 1890s there was no unemployment benefit and no old age pensions. Hundreds of thousands of artisans were out of work. They were sleeping six on a bench on the Embankment between Temple and Blackfriars; they huddled together for warmth in the arches of Blackfriars Bridge; they were sleeping by the score in Spitalfields graveyard and in the shop doors of Liverpool Street. Frank Collier tells how the Salvation Army began to investigate this problem. And on a single evening in June 1890 there were in the middle of the night 368 men sleeping out in the single mile between Westminster and Blackfriars, living through the hell of empty days on a pennyworth of bread and a pennyworth of soup per day.

When I went to my first and only parish in Renfrew in the early thirties, we were almost at once plunged into that terrible depression which hit the world in the middle thirties, and of my twenty-seven elders nineteen were unemployed. It was then that I saw men's skill rotting in idleness. It was then that I knew what Sir Henry Arthur Jones the philosopher meant when he said that the saddest words in all Shakespeare are: 'Othello's occupation's gone.' This is something which in a Christian country must never happen again. It is the racial memory of these days which produced and produces things like restrictive practices and the failure to work all out. There is the unconscious memory and the unconscious fear that these workless days might come back.

ii. There is next *the right of a man to a living wage*. Again in 1890—which, mark you, is still within the lifetime of people still alive—Richard Collier quotes an instance of a mother and two children under nine working sixteen hours a day to produce 1,000 matchboxes for a wage of 1s. 5¾d. All right—that cannot happen now—but it happened—and it takes more than one generation to eradicate the memory of that.

iii. There is *the right of a man to reasonable working conditions*. This was something which eighty years ago did not enter into an employer's calculations. Richard Collier tells of how matches were made at that time to sell at a penny per dozen boxes. At that price they had to be made of yellow phosphorus, of which three grains are lethal. The workers dipped the matches in the phosphorus and the operation put them in peril of their lives. They would touch their faces. They would think that they had toothache. It was phosphorus attacking the jaw. 'Soon the whole side of the face turned green, then black, discharging foul-smelling pus. This was "phossy jaw"—necrosis of the bone—and the one outcome was death.' In a workshop in which phosphorus was used, if the light was put out—I quote—'in the eerie darkness, the victim's jaw, even her hands, glowed greenish-white like a spectre's, as the phosphorus rotted her while she lived'—and people were brought to see this as a sight. You cannot do that to people without leaving this racial memory which it will take generations to remove. When we remember the nineteenth century, the wonder is, not that industrial relations can be difficult, but that they are as good as they are. When people who were treated like that find themselves in a position to defend themselves and to have their demands met, no one can blame them for taking the chance. The simple fact is that it is impossible to build an industrial community on an industrial ethic which is unchristian. Our forefathers did just that, and it is our task to mend the situation—but first we must understand it.

But now we must bring the matter home. What is work to me? What place has it in my life? What ought work to be to me? What place ought it to have in my life?

It can be that my work is everything, and that for it I live. Carlyle said: 'Blessed is he who has found his work; let him ask no further blessedness.' Sir Henry Coward the musician said at the end of his career that there was no reason to thank or congratulate him on his work, because all his life he had been paid for doing the work that he would gladly have paid to be allowed to do. Paul Tournier the great doctor said that every doctor must feel that he is a collaborator with God. A man can find God and life in his work. You remember Kipling's M'Andrew, the Scots engineer down in the bowels of the ship who tended his engines and thought of God:

From coupler-flange to spindle-guide I see thy hand, O God,
Predestination in the stride o' yon connectin' rod.

These and such as these find real life in their work. But that is far from being true of everyone. You remember how Robert Louis Stevenson tells in his *Inland Voyage* about the man who drove the hotel bus at Maubeuge: the man said: 'Here I am. I drive to the station—well—and then I drive back to the hotel; and so on every day all the week round. My God, is that life?' Or you remember Charles Lamb, for thirty-three long years a clerk in the East India Company offices, as he talks of

> *the dry drudgery of the desk's dead wood.*

For long enough now Christian ethics has been piously teaching that in our everyday work we must find our joy, our pride, our self-satisfaction, our self-fulfilment. We have been comfortably quoting John Keble:

> *The trivial round, the common task,*
> *Would furnish all we ought to ask;*
> *Room to deny ourselves; a road*
> *To bring us, daily, nearer God.*

It is time that we stopped talking pious platitudes and took a fresh look at our philosophy of work. Of course, it is still possible for a man to find his life in his work. A minister of the gospel can do so. As Peter Green used to say: 'Had I nine lives like a cat, I should have been a parish priest every time.' A doctor, a teacher, an artist, a craftsman, a motor mechanic who has the thrill of seeing a recalcitrant engine bursting into life—this is all right. But this is not by any means all. In the first place, I doubt if more than 10 per cent of people really choose what they are going to do. They leave the school, and they take the first thing that comes to hand—not because they want to, but because they have to. In the second place, the more developed industry becomes, the more automation takes over, the cleverer we become, the more jobs there are in which a man is a machine-minder, a presser of buttons, a manipulator of switches, a doer of one repetitive action as the article which is taking shape glides past him on the conveyor belt. The plain fact is—we cannot find life in that kind of existence. And it is going to become commoner and commoner. The machine replaces the craftsman; an automatic process replaces individual skill; and a man is left doing things in which it is not possible to take a pride.

We have then frankly to admit that under modern conditions a man's work may well be the process by which he earns a living for himself and for his family—and nothing more. And the consequence is that nowadays there are many, an increasing number, who will have to find their real life outside their work.

There are plenty of people who have already solved this problem. There are men who earn a living through the day and who come alive when they sing in a choir or act in a dramatic society in the evening. There are people who through the day earn so much money, and then come home to find life in a Boy's Brigade or a Scout Company, in work for epileptics or spastics, or for the old or the homeless. There are people who have a hobby which is their life.

There are any number of people who have, so to speak, lived double lives. Charles Lamb was the slave of his desk in the office, but he escaped to write the essays the world still reads. C. L. Dodgson was teaching mathematics and writing textbooks, *An Elementary Treatise on Determinants* or *Curiosa Mathematica*, but he was writing *Alice in Wonderland* at the same time. There are people who have a sphere of service or of interest or of art into which they can escape and live.

But there are others who have not, who cannot see beyond the picture house, the television set, the bingo hall, the football match—all good enough things but not things in which a man can invest his life. So certain things are needed.

i. What we are really saying is that a situation is arising when a man needs education for leisure as much as he needs education for work. This must mean the rebirth of education, so that education does not only teach the things necessary to make a living, but also the things which make men able to live.

There is a sense in which education has broken down. There are areas with schools out of which a child will come never having written one single line in answer to any question, unable to put a paragraph together on paper. There are levels of education out of which the child will come with no reading desire other than the strip cartoon or the comic.

When G. K. Chesterton was a child he had a cardboard toy theatre with cut-out characters. One of the characters was a man with a golden key; he never could remember what character that man with the golden key represented; but that character was always identified in his mind with his father, whom he saw as a man with a golden key who unlocked all sorts of doors leading to all sorts of wonderful things. The dream of education is that education should be a golden key to unlock the doors, not simply to the skills which are necessary to make a living, but to the things of the human spirit, of art, of music, of drama, by which men and women will find life.

ii. Man has a body as well as a mind; and a good deal of the juvenile delinquency which exists is due to men forgetting this fact. It is incredible that many new towns were planned in which there was literally nothing to do; and in which if there was any grass the only thing allowed on it was a notice telling you to keep off it. Eric Fromm the psychologist has said quite truly that everyone—especially a young person—has in him a certain dynamism, a certain almost crude life force, and if that force, that energy, is not directed towards life, it will certainly be directed into destruction. *Destruction is the outcome of unlived life.* We cannot put a young person in a concrete desert with nothing to do, or in the end he will heave a brick through a window or start a fight through sheer boredom. In the new society there must be plenty to do when the hours of work are done.

iii. In the new world, in which the time after work matters so much, the church must become the centre of the community. Of course, a church is a place where men praise and pray, but a church should be far more than that; the church should be the place to which men turn to find the satisfaction of every honest need in life. It is one of the great truths that the better we know a person the more deeply and truly we can worship with him. We can pray best with the man with whom we have played best. The man beside us in church should not be a holy stranger but a living friend.

Long ago, George Bernard Shaw of all people wrote a piece about the church. It is obviously dated now, but in principle it remains the same:

> If some enterprising clergyman with a cure of souls in the slums were to hoist a board over his church door with the following inscription: Here men and women after working hours may dance without getting drunk on Fridays; hear good music on Saturdays; pray on Sundays; discuss public affairs without molestation from the police on Mondays; have the building for any honest purpose they choose on Tuesdays; bring the children for games, amusing drill and romps on Wednesdays; and volunteer for a thorough scrubbing down of the place on Thursdays, he could reform the whole neighbourhood.

The church with the seven-day open door must be part of the new era.

iv. One last thing—we have seen that work can be the biggest thing in life, but that for many life will need to begin after the day's work is done. We have been suggesting ways in which this new leisure can be and must be used; but we cannot leave it there. So far our suggestions have been basically selfish. The one thing that could give meaning to life is service —the service of the community. If the mature would remember what they could do for the young, from teaching them judo to teaching them the Bible; if the young would remember what young hands can do for the lonely, the aged and the helpless; if the strong would remember the weak, and if those who have too much would remember those who have too little; if there was an inbuilt obligation to service there would

104

be no problem at all, for it is in living for others that a man finds life for himself.

Originally it was at this point that this lecture ended. But not long after it had been televised it was pointed out to me by a university colleague whose views I respect, and who had been leading a discussion group, that it had one basic omission. All through it I have assumed as a first principle that work is an essential part of life, that the Christian ethic presupposes the fact that a man will work. But—I was challenged—what about those who have dropped out from work, or who wish to do so? And I do not mean those who have dropped out through laziness, or through unwillingness to work, or through inability to work. I am not thinking of the person who, without disrespect, can be called the professional lay-about. I am thinking about the person who feels that on nothing less than conscientious grounds he is under obligation to drop out, the person whose decision to drop out is in its own way a religious decision.

There are beyond any doubt young people who feel what is far more than a resentment against society. They feel that society is such that they cannot take part in it. Society, they say, is literally and spiritually polluted. Society is utterly materialised. Society, to use the common phrase, is a rat race. Society grows rich on the manufacture of armaments and the like. Society is the battle of the *have's* to avoid sharing with the *have not's*, to cling on to their possessions and to retain their vested interests at all costs. There are people who honestly and sincerely feel that they are compelled to drop out of such a society. It is not because they are lazy spongers that they opt out; it is because they feel intensely that they do not want to be involved in that which society has become and will become. What have we to say to people like that?

i. It has to be said that anything like a complete drop-out is, in fact, an impossibility. Whether society is good or bad, a man cannot do without it. He has to use the services with which society supplies him. Somehow he has to eat and to live and he depends on society to enable him to do so. In the nature of things we have to use the services which society implies, even to accepting support from the society for which we refuse to work. Completely to opt out of society is not possible. We may disapprove of society, but we cannot sever ourselves completely from it.

ii. One of the great questions in regard to this is—drop out into what? Is the drop-out to be a drop-out into a completely non-productive, negative form of life, where endless talk takes the place of action? Very few would drop out, say, into a monastic order, where with discipline and devotion a man might withdraw from society to pray for the society from which he had withdrawn. Is the drop-out to be from all that the world calls a career into some form of service, the rewards of which are in material terms negligible, but the effect of which is to relieve, as far as we can relieve them, the hunger and the pain and the sorrow of the world? Would a man drop out of life in order in some way to dedicate his life to the end of racialism, the end of war, the end of poverty? This is the acid test. To drop out into utter inactivity is to fail in one's obligation as a human being to other human beings. Protest can often be right; this kind of abdication can hardly ever be right. A man does not shed his responsibilities by ignoring them. A man may deny that he has any obligation to an effete and polluted society; he cannot deny his obligation to humanity.

iii. What I have just said involves and implies something else. A man of really conscientious mind has to decide what he can do and what he can not do. He may come to the conclusion that the society in which he lives is a rotten society from top to bottom. But this does not mean that there are not many things in this society which a man can do without involving himself in the pollution of society, and in doing which he may be the means of purifying—or it might be destroying—this society. The doctor, the social worker, the youth leader, often the teacher, the parson are often just as incensed at society as the man who has decided to drop out. The man who drops out has to ask himself if the best way to register his protest is to do nothing. Can you really build life on a negative? Is withdrawal the only way? Is there literally nowhere in society where a man can keep his heart pure and his hands clean? Is there nowhere he can strike a blow for the ideals in which he so intensely believes?

Suppose a person does feel that society is corrupt and materialised and inhuman, suppose that he does feel that he must withdraw from an industrialised society, must he include in his sweeping condemnation the shepherd with his sheep, the ploughman with his plough, the nurse with her patients, the surgeon bringing men back from death to life, the priest slaving his life out in some slum parish? I am not able to believe that there is absolutely nothing that the idealist can find to do. I am quite certain that he can find something to do which will not wound his conscience or outrage his principles.

iv. It would be quite wrong to level the charge against all who drop out, but it is true that many who drop out involve themselves in practices which are more than doubtful. A man may feel so distressed about the evils of society that he drops out from it, and may at the same time involve himself in the ruinous experiments of drug-taking. He may wish to end war and at the same time he may eagerly take part in demonstrations which are in themselves small wars. He may talk about love, and he may be a source of very grave anxiety to those who have loved him most and to those to whom he owes the greatest debt of love. It is very hard to see how ideals which are so high that they compel a man to abandon society can lead him to the kind of life which some of such people have chosen to live.

Further, it is a disturbing fact that there is an element of waste in all this. It often happens that those who drop out from society are people of considerable intellectual ability. They are often young people of very great gifts and of very high potential. Unquestionably, such people have a genuine distress in face of the kind of society by which they are surrounded. If that is so, it would be to be expected that their first desire would be to change it. And the only way to change society is from the inside. It is easy to understand the reformer, the rebel, the revolutionary, even the wrecker. It is much more difficult to understand the person whose protest consists in doing nothing. A man on strike certainly withdraws his labour, but he only does so that the conditions of his labour may be reformed and improved, if not for himself, then certainly for those who are to come after him.

v. One other simple thing remains to be said. If a person drops out from the life of society, all the chances are that in the end he will find himself fighting one of the greatest enemies of human life—boredom. There comes a time in life when work of some kind becomes a human necessity. There are many definitions of man, and in the end it may well be true to say that man is naturally a working animal. In every life there are times for doing nothing. It might well be an excellent thing if at some time in every man's life there was such a period; but over the years man was meant to do something, and in the end he will not be happy unless he does.

It would be impossible to question the ideals and the sincerity of many of those who drop out from society. But I do not think that they have chosen the right way, because I do not think that life can be built on a negative, and I do not think that a permanent protest can be based on doing nothing, and I believe that man is better to be even the active enemy of society than the passive abandoner of society.

CHAPTER SIX

The Christian View of Pleasure

There are few things harder to define than pleasure. The same thing can be a delight to one person and a penance to another. There is in pleasure a completely subjective element. To one person one kind of food is appetising and desirable, to another person the very same thing is nauseating. One kind of music will thrill one person and will appear to another person only an unpleasant noise. One person will enjoy games and sport; another person will think them a childish waste of time. One person will read avidly a certain kind of book; another person will find the same kind of book almost unreadable. One person will love travel; another person will find it an exhausting weariness. Pleasure varies from person to person—but there must be some kind of principle behind all the variation.

The simplest thing to say is that pleasure is the opposite of work, but that will hardly do. In the first place, there are people who are never happier than when they are at their work. Their work is a joy to them. Take it away and you would take from them that which in life they enjoy most of all. And secondly, there are many pleasures which involve a great deal of hard work. Many a man works harder at some game at which he wants to excel than at his day's work. Many a man puts a great deal of thought and time and effort into his hobby. There are people whose pleasures look very like hard labour.

We may go a step further. We may say that the effort which pleasure involves is effort which is voluntarily made, and which is made for the sake of no material reward. For instance, a man might spend a great deal of time and thought and effort and money building up a stamp collection in which he found delight; that would be pleasure. But, if he stopped stamp-collecting and started stamp-dealing, he would be doing much the same kind of things, but it would be work. A man may spend a great deal of time and money on a game, and so long as it is a game it will be pleasure. But he may decide to become a professional; he may decide to make his living by that game. In that case he will be doing much the same kind of things, but it will be work. It is then true that the absolutely voluntary nature of the activity is an essential part of pleasure.

But still another step must be taken. A man may spend a great deal of time and thought and money on some activity; it may be quite voluntary; it may have no material reward. But it may not be in the normal sense of the word pleasure. For instance, a man may give a great deal of time to church work, to youth work, to social service. He does it voluntarily; he does it for no material reward; but that is not what we normally mean by pleasure.

So we have to come back to the essential meaning of the word. Pleasure is that which is *pleasant*; and that which is pleasant is that which is *pleasing*. Pleasure is that which a man does simply and solely to please himself. Pleasure is what a man does when he does what he likes. He is not doing it because he has to; he is not doing it to earn money and to support his family; he is not doing it to be of help and service to others; he is doing it for no other reason than that he likes doing it.

We no sooner begin to think of pleasure than we remember that there have often been Christians to whom pleasure is a bad word. There were those who thought the same long before Christianity came into the world. Antisthenes the Cynic philosopher once said that he would rather be mad than pleased, that he would prefer madness to pleasure. There have been those who would have said that there was no such thing as a good pleasure, if pleasure is taken as referring to anything in this world.

The monks and the hermits of the fourth and fifth centuries were like that. H. B. Workman describes them in his book, *The Evolution of the Monastic Ideal.* They made a cult of discomfort. They trained themselves to do without food. A Cilician monk called Conon existed for thirty years on one meal a week. They trained themselves to do without sleep. Adolus never slept except the three hours before dawn. Sisoes spent the night on a jutting crag so that if he fell asleep, he would pitch to his death. Pachomius never lay down, but slept, when he did sleep, standing in his cell. Some lived on grass; some lived in cells so small that they could neither stand up nor lie down. Some were famous for their 'fleshlessness'. It was said of Macarius that 'for seven years he ate nothing cooked by fire', so that 'the bones of his face stood out naked beyond the wont of men'.

They made a cult of filth. The dirtier they were, the holier they were. It was said of Simeon Stylites, as a mark of great holiness, that his body 'dropped vermin as he walked'. Jerome wrote to Paula: 'Why should Paula add fuel to a sleeping fire by taking a bath?' And Paula replied: 'A clean body and a clean dress mean an unclean soul.' Anthony never changed his vest or washed his feet. The great Roman lady Melania boasted that after her conversion she never allowed water to touch her, except the tips of her fingers, in spite of her doctor's advice.

They made a cult of killing all human emotion and all human relationships. There is nothing uglier than their view of the relationship between men and women. Augustine would never see any woman except in the presence of a third party. An Egyptian monk Pior was ordered by his superior to see his sister. He obeyed, but he kept his eyes shut tight all the time he was in his sister's presence. A dying nun refused to see her brother. Melania, to whom we have already referred, lost her husband and two of her three sons in one week. Her reaction

111

was to thank God: 'More easily can I serve thee, O Lord, in that thou hast relieved me of so great a burden.' When Paula was about to enter the convent, her children wept and besought her not to leave them. 'She raised her eyes to heaven, and overcame her love for her children by her love for God. She knew herself no longer a mother.' A certain Mucius entered a convent with his eight-year-old son. They were separated. To test Mucius the boy was systematically beaten. 'The love of Christ conquered, nor did he grieve over the lad's injuries.' One day when the lad was in tears, Mucius was ordered to throw him into the river. And 'this new Abraham' would have done so, had the monks not stopped him.

It is easy to see what people like that would have thought of the word pleasure. And that tradition has never wholly died.

It took England a very long time to escape from the Puritan tradition. The best account of Puritan England is still to be found in Chapter 8 of John Richard Green's *A Short History of the English People* and in the second chapter of Thomas Babington Macaulay's *The History of England from the Accession of James the Second*.

The publication of the Authorised Version of the Bible did something to England. 'Theology', said Grotius, 'rules there.' 'There is great abundance of theologians in England,' Casaubon said to a friend. 'All point their studies in that direction.' As J. R. Green put it: 'The whole nation became, in fact, a church.' But at first there might be gravity and solemnity and seriousness, but there was no gloom. Colonel Hutchinson was one of the people who signed the death warrant of Charles the First; he was a Cromwellian and a Puritan. His wife left a most beautiful biography of him, which was published early in the nineteenth century. Hutchinson was serious enough, but he was expert in hawking, in fencing and in dancing. He loved 'gravings, sculptures and all the liberal arts'. 'He had a great love for music, and often diverted himself on a viol, on which he played masterly.' John Milton and John Milton's father were Puritans. But John Milton's father composed madrigals to Oriana. He saw to it that his son knew French and Italian as well as Latin, Greek and Hebrew. John Milton played the lute and the organ, and he could admit to loving the theatre of Shakespeare and Ben Jonson.

Early Puritanism was not what Puritanism was to become. More and more the seriousness and the gravity turned to gloom. More and more the elect stressed and felt their difference from the world. As J. R. Green puts it: 'Humour, the faculty which above all corrects exaggeration and extravagance, died away before the new stress and strain of existence.' A grim legalism descended on life. 'The godly man learned to shrink from a surplice, or a mince-pie at Christmas, as he shrank from impurity or a lie.'

Macaulay tells how the Book of Common Prayer was banned from public and even from private use. 'It was a crime in a child to read by the bedside of a sick parent one of those beautiful collects which had soothed the griefs of forty generations of Christians.' Any picture which showed Jesus or Mary was burned. Works of art and beautiful churches were brutally defaced. All public amusements were prohibited and an ordinance was passed that every Maypole in England should be hewn down. All theatrical shows were banned. Playhouses were dismantled, spectators fined, and actors whipped at the cart's tail. Rope-dancing, puppet-shows, bowls, horse-racing, wrestling-matches, games on the village green were all banished from life. The Long Parliament of 1644 put an end to Christmas Day and enacted that 25th December should be observed as a national fast, on which men bemoaned the sins their fathers had previously committed on that day 'by romping under the mistletoe, eating boar's head, and drinking ale flavoured with roasted apples'. Fiddlers were put in the stocks; dancing and hockey on the village green were ended. It was when he was engaged on what he called 'the ungodly practice' of playing tipcat that the voice came to Bunyan: 'Wilt thou leave thy sins and go to Heaven, or have thy sins and go to Hell?' Bell-ringing and tipcat had become crimes of the first magnitude.

Henry Graham's *Social Life of Scotland in the Eighteenth Century* provides a picture at least as gloomy, especially in the chapter on religious and ecclesiastical life. In 1715 a Dumfriesshire Presbytery spent months investigating the charge against a minister that on a printing machine which he had in his manse he had printed copies of a 'profane' song called 'Maggie Lauder'. The Presbytery of Edinburgh denounced those who 'immediately before public worship, and then after it was over, take recreation in walking in the fields, links, meadows and other places, and by entering taverns, ale-houses and milk-houses, drink tipple, or otherwise spend any part thereof, or despise and profane the Sabbath by giving or receiving social visits, or by idly gazing out of windows beholding vanities abroad'. Simply to talk in the street, to go for a walk, to pay a visit, even to look out of the window had become a sin.

In Scotland in the eighteenth century one of the popular institutions was the 'penny wedding'. The people were very poor, and on the occasion of a wedding all contributed a very small sum that there might be an entertainment, especially an entertainment with dancing. In 1715 the Kirk Session of Morton in Dumfriesshire condemned the penny weddings. It talks about 'the great abuse that is committing at wedding dinners, and in particular by promiscuous dancing betwixt young men and women, which is most abominable, not to be practised in a land of light, and condemned of former time of Presbytery as not only unnecessary but sensual, being only an inlet of lust and provocation to uncleanness through the corruptions of men and women in this loose and degenerate age, wherein the devil seems to be raging by a spirit of uncleanness and profanity, making such practices an occasion to the flesh, and thereby drawing men and women to dishonour God, ruin their own souls, and cast reproach upon the holy ways of religion'. Anyone taking part in a penny wedding was to be fined by the church and publicly rebuked at the church service. To people with minds like that any entertainment in which men and women shared was an evil thing.

A certain Mr John Willison was a popular preacher and writer in those days. He gave advice to his people about how they must live so as not to forget God. When they put on their clothes, they must think of the nakedness of their souls and for the need of the robes of imputed righteousness. When they comb their head they must think of their sins, which are more than the hairs thereof. When they sit at supper, they must think of the joy of some day supping with Abraham, Isaac and Jacob. As they see themselves stripped of clothing, as they prepare for bed, they must think that they came naked into the world and that they will leave it naked. And, as they cover themselves with the blankets, they must think of lying in the cold grave and being covered with the earth.

There was little room for pleasure in a day spent in thoughts like that.

It must have been desperately hard to be a child in those days. John Wesley drew up the rules for his famous school at Kingswood near Bristol. No games whatever were to be allowed in the school. 'He who plays when he is a child will play when he is a man'—and that is not to be thought of. There were no holidays at all. From the day he entered the school until the day he left it, the child had no holiday. All in the school, adults and children alike, rose at four in the morning. The first hour was spent in reading and meditation, in singing and in prayer. On Fridays they fasted until three o'clock in the afternoon. After thirty-five years of it Wesley wrote in his diary: 'The children ought never to play, but they do every day, and even in the school. They run about in the wood, and mix and even fight with the colliers' children . . . They are not religious: they have not the power and hardly the form of it.' W. M. Macgregor, telling of this in his book, *The Making of a Preacher*, wonders at any man trying to

115

lead his fellow men to God and understanding them so little!

George Whitefield recounts in his *Journals* an incident which happened on board the ship on which he was sailing to America:

Had a good instance of the benefit of breaking children's wills betimes. Last night, going between decks (as I do every night) to visit the sick and to examine my people, I asked one of the women to bid her little boy say his prayers. She answered his elder sister would, but she could not make him. Upon this I bid the child kneel down before me, but he would not, till I took hold of his two feet and forced him down. I then bid him say the Lord's Prayer (being informed by his mother he could say it if he would), but he obstinately refused, till at last, after I had given him several blows, he said his prayer as well as could be expected and I gave him some figs for a reward.

Susannah Wesley said about bringing up children: 'The first thing to be done is to conquer their will . . . I insist on conquering the will of children betimes.'

When we remember this kind of attitude, we can very easily see how the church at least in some of its parts inherited a suspicion of pleasure, and how pleasure came to be looked on as something which is wrong as such. And to this day there are still lingering remnants of this attitude.

It would be true to say that a man is known by his pleasures, and so is a society. The things which a man enjoys will provide a clear indication of his character, and the things which it calls sport will reveal the character of a nation. It will then be important to look at the pleasures of that Roman society to which the Christian ethic was first preached.

The basic fact in the whole situation was that by the time Christianity entered the world Rome was mistress of the world, and the Roman citizen was convinced that work was beneath him. The work of the world, as far as he was concerned, was done by slaves. This meant that in Rome there were about

150,000 people who had literally nothing to do; and there were another 100,000 whose work was finished by noon. Some safety-valve had to be found for this mass of people; somehow they had to be kept fed and amused. Hence there came the famous phrase that all that the populace now wanted was 'bread and circuses' (Juvenal, *Satires* 10.77-81). Fronto said that the Roman populace was absorbed in two things—food and the shows.

It has been pointed out that Rome had more public holidays than any society in history has ever had. On these public holidays everything stopped, and the populace thronged to state-provided amusements. In the time of Augustus, 66 days were public holidays each year; in the time of Tiberius, 87; in the time of Marcus Aurelius, 135; in the fourth century, 175. When the Colosseum was dedicated under Titus, there were 100 consecutive days of shows and holidays. When Trajan celebrated his Dacian triumph there were 123 consecutive days of public holiday and entertainment. The hardest work that the Roman did was his pursuit of pleasure. Let us then see what these pleasures were.

There have been few times in history with such a passion for gambling. Juvenal said that it was not a purse that men brought to the gambling tables; it was a treasure chest. Nero, Suetonius tells us, gambled at the rate of the equivalent of £4,000 on each pip of the dice, for dicing was the favourite game. At a dinner-party Augustus usually presented each guest with £10 so that, if he so wished, the guest could gamble to pass the time.

Equally, there can have been few ages in history so dedicated to gluttony. By this time the Romans had formed the habit of taking emetics before a meal, and even between courses, to enjoy the food better. Vitellius held power for only a few months during the chaos which followed the death of Nero. He served a dish in a platter called The Shield of Minerva. Suetonius says: 'In this he mingled the livers of pike, the brains of pheasants and peacocks, the tongues of flamingoes, the milt of lampreys.' When Vitellius entered Rome and assumed for his brief space the imperial power, his brother gave a banquet, at which there were served two thousand fish and seven thousand birds. Seneca (*Moral Letters* 95.15-29) compares the modern luxury with the old Spartan fare. Nowadays, he says, it is not a question of finding dishes to satisfy the appetite but rather to arouse it. Countless sauces are devised to whet men's gluttony. Food was once nourishment for a man; now it is a further burden to an already overburdened stomach. Hence the characteristic paleness, the trembling of wine-sodden muscles, the repulsive thinness due to indigestion rather than to hunger; hence the dropsy; hence the belly grown to a paunch by repeatedly taking more than it can hold; hence the yellow jaundice; the body rotting inwardly; the thickened and stiffened joints . . . The halls of the professor and scholar are empty, but the restaurants are besieged with crowds. There is a medley of bakers and a scurry of waiters. 'How many are kept busy to humour a single belly!' And note it is not a Christian preacher but a Stoic philosopher who is responsible for this indictment. There is a curious resemblance between that world and the world of the latter half of the twentieth century, a world of betting-shops and plush restaurants, a world in which abject poverty and the lushest kind of wealth existed side by side.

It was the age of the degeneration of the theatre. The theatre had become sexual, bawdy and depraved. But it had become something worse. It had become cruel. Many of the plays were about some criminal character and his exploits. In many cases the criminal in the play was played by an actual criminal. And the play ended with the criminal on the stage being crucified or torn limb from limb in the full sight of the audience.

It was the great age of chariot-racing. The greatest of the arenas was the Circus Maximus which was about two hundred yards long and about sixty yards wide; it had room for

385,000 spectators. The race was usually seven laps. The chariots might have up to eight or ten horses. This meant that the chariots went fourteen times round the turning-posts, and it was there that what one writer called 'the bloody shipwreck' could happen, for the drivers drove standing in the chariot with the reins wrapped round their bodies, and the flying wheels and the trampling hooves at the turning-points caused many a disaster. The public and even the Emperors were fanatical supporters of the whites or the blues or the greens or the reds. A charioteer could finish up a millionaire. Diocles rode 4,257 races and won 1,462 victories and retired with £375,000. It was not only the prospect of disaster that lured in the crowds; it was the betting in which the millionaire betted in his thousands and the man on the dole staked his last penny. There was even a transfer system whereby the most famous riders were lured away from one faction to another. Chariot-racing in Rome and big-time sport today bear a close resemblance, not least in the way that the financial rewards of sport make nonsense of all real values.

It was, as all the world knows, the age of the gladiatorial games. It was at these that the people received their greatest thrill. The rag man in Petronius' story looks forward to the games which Titus is going to give. 'He'll give us cold steel and no shrinking, and a good bit of butchery in full view of the arena.' That 'carnival of blood' had a strange fascination. Alypius, the friend of Augustine, gave up the games when he became a Christian, but on one occasion his friends dragged him to the arena with them. At first he held his hands over his eyes and refused to look; but the atmosphere got him, and soon he was shouting and swaying and roaring with the rest. There were the Samnites who fought with a great shield and a short sword; there were the Thracians who fought with a little shield and a long curved scimitar; there were the heavy-armed myrmilliones, so called from the fish-badge on their helmets; there were the *retiarii*, the net men, who fought with net and trident; there were the horsemen with their long lances, and the charioteers with the wheels of the chariots with projecting scythe-like blades.

The numbers of the gladiators constantly grew. Julius Caesar had 320 pairs of gladiators; Augustus claimed to have put 10,000 men into the arena. At Trajan's Dacian games 4,941 pairs of gladiators fought in under 120 days. Sometimes they fought each other. Sometimes they fought with beasts. When Titus dedicated his great amphitheatre in AD 80, 5,000 animals were exhibited as shows and more than 9,000 were killed. And in Trajan's Dacian triumph in AD 107, 11,000 animals were killed.

Sometimes the gladiators were slaves; sometimes they were criminals; sometimes they were prisoners captured in war; sometimes they were men who fought because they wanted to. Sometimes a great gladiator fought for years and retired wealthy and honoured. The great ambition of a gladiator was some day to be presented with the wooden sword which signified honourable retirement. Then he would hang up his armour in the temple of Hercules and maybe retire to a little country estate and live to see his son become a citizen—and sometimes he came back to the arena, for there were gladiators who had fighting in their blood.

There were even artificial sea-battles. Artificial lakes, sometimes 1,800 feet long and 2,000 feet wide, were dug out and flooded; and there were sea-fights in which as many as 19,000 marines took part.

The Christian ethic first came to a society which was thrilled by murder in the name of sport. And it is the mark of the power of the Christian ethic that, while the gambling and the gluttony and the pornography continue, the bloodthirsty cruelty is gone.

It is now time to see if we can lay down certain principles by which pleasures may be judged. We can approach this from two different angles. We can approach it from the *negative* angle, and we can lay down certain principles on which certain things have to be rejected; and we can approach it from the *positive* angle, and we can lay down certain tests which a true pleasure must satisfy.

i. No pleasure can be right if its effects on the person who indulges in it are harmful. There are pleasures which can injure a man's body and which in the end can have a permanent ill-effect on his health. There are pleasures which can coarsen a man's moral fibre. There are pleasures which can weaken a man's character and lower his resistance power against that which is wrong. Any pleasure which leaves a man less physically fit, less mentally alert, less morally sensitive is wrong.

There are obvious instances of this. The excessive use of alcohol lowers a man's power of self-control and renders him liable to do things which he would not have done if he had been soberly master of himself. The taking of drugs and stimulants can end in leaving a man a physical and mental wreck. Over-indulgence in eating and drinking can leave a man a burden to himself, with his physical fitness seriously impaired. Promiscuous sexual relationships can leave a man with the most tragic of diseases, diseases which will not only ruin his own life, but will descend to any children he may beget.

One of the simplest tests of pleasure is: What does it do to the man who indulges in it? If it is actively harmful, or even if it has a built-in risk in it, it cannot be right.

ii. No pleasure can be right if its effect on others is harmful. There are pleasures which can result in the corruption of other people, either physically or morally. To teach others to do wrong, to invite them to do so, or to make it easier for them to do so, cannot be right. It is no small sin to teach another to sin. When Burns went to Irvine to learn flax-dressing he met a man whose influence was altogether bad. Afterwards he said of him: 'His friendship did me a mischief.' It is precisely this that Jesus unsparingly condemned. 'Whoever causes one of these little ones who believe in me to sin, it would be better for him to have a great millstone fastened round his neck and to be drowned in the depth of the sea. Woe to the world for temptations to sin! For it is necessary that temptations come, but woe to the man by whom the temptation comes!' (Matthew 18.6,7). If Jesus is right it is easier for a man to be forgiven for his own sins than it is for him to be forgiven for the sins which he taught to others. A man may have a certain right to ruin his own life; he has no right at all to ruin the life of someone else.

A person always needs the first impulse to sin. True, that impulse will often come from within his own heart. But almost always it needs someone's push to turn the inner desire into outer action. And tragically often the wrong thing can be given a spurious attraction. To take drugs can be painted as adventurous and free. An illicit relationship can be presented as a beautiful friendship. Experiment with things which experience has proved to be disastrous can be looked on as the assertion of freedom. To lead or persuade or seduce someone else into any kind of conduct which is hurtful and harmful is a grave and terrible responsibility.

iii. A pleasure which becomes an addiction can never be right. The formation of a habit is one of the most terrifying things in life. The first time a person does a wrong thing he does it with hesitation and with difficulty. There are many forms of self-indulgence which are actually unpleasant when they are first tried, but which in the end can become a tyranny. The second time the thing is done it will be easier, and so on. The initial unpleasantness will give place to pleasure, and the day will come when a man discovers that he cannot do without the thing. It has become an addiction. One of the old Greeks said that there were only two questions about any pleasure: 'Do I possess it?' or, 'Am I possessed by it?' 'Do I control it?' or, 'Does it control me?' The minute a man feels that some pleasure is gripping him in such a way that he cannot do without it, he will be well advised to break it before it breaks him. Addiction can happen with quite ordinary things like tobacco; it can happen with more serious things like alcohol; it can happen with drugs, so that a man becomes 'hooked' on some drug, the slave of the evil thing. It is better to have nothing to do with a pleasure which is liable to become an addiction. It is essential, the moment we become aware of the growing addiction, to stop.

iv. A pleasure is wrong, if to enjoy it the essentials of life have to take less than their proper place. A pleasure can cost too much, even if it is a good thing in itself. A man may spend on a game time and money which should have gone to his home and family. A man may practise a public generosity which leaves too little for his own home. A man may be so active in the service of the community, of youth, even of the church, that he has too little time left for his own wife and his own children. Anything in life that gets out of proportion is wrong. Whenever any pleasure annexes time and money which should have gone to things and to people in life of even greater importance, then, however fine it is in itself, it is wrong.

v. Any pleasure which can be a source of danger to others must be very carefully thought about. Here we are back at Paul's insistence that he will eat and drink nothing which might cause his brother man to fall into error (Romans 14. 21; 1 Corinthians 8.13). He will put an obstacle in no man's way (2 Corinthians 6,3). This is not something on which we can lay down definite rules and regulations. It is something for a man's own conscience to decide within the context of the life that he has to live. But a man is a selfish man if he insists for his own pleasure on that which may ruin his brother.

vi. We may end this series of principles with what is the most far-reaching test of all. *The ultimate test of any pleasure is, does it, or does it not, bring regret to follow, and that pleasure which brings regret is wrong.* Epicurus was one of the very few philosophers who declared that pleasure is the supreme good in life. And we use the word *epicurean* to describe a person who is a devotee of pleasure. But when we do so, we do grave injustice to Epicurus. For Epicurus always insisted that it is essential to take the long view of pleasure, that it is essential to ask, not, what does this feel like just now? but, what will this feel like in the time to come? Epicurus was therefore himself the least epicurean of persons. He believed in a diet of bread and water, for such a diet has no ill consequences to follow. He believed in justice, in honour, in honesty, in chastity and in fidelity, for only when life is lived in these things are there no regrets. Epicurus believed that, if you do make pleasure the supreme good in life, you must take the long view of pleasure.

This is the final guide. We must always ask, not simply, will I enjoy this at this moment? but also, how will I feel about this in time to come? This even the prudent man of the world will ask, but the Christian will ask not only what the thing will feel like in time to come, but also what it will feel like in eternity to come. And if that be so, the supreme test of pleasure is, can it bear the scrutiny of God?

We now turn to the positive side of the matter, and we try to lay down certain principles regarding the Christian view of pleasure.

i. *Pleasure is a necessary element in life, because, if there is no pleasure, one essential part of the total personality of a man is not being satisfied.* Certainly, in life there is the basic need to work; but equally certainly, there is the basic need to play. The desire to play is instinctive. No one needs to teach animals to play. No one needs to teach children to play. Long before they come to the games which have their special rules and which a child has to be taught, children have invented their own games and their own play. 'All work and no play makes Jack a dull boy,' the proverb says. It does not only make him a dull boy; it makes him an unnatural boy as well.

Life must have its work, and equally life must have its leisure. Leisure can on occasion mean doing nothing, but more often leisure means doing things. Man has two instincts. He has the gregarious instinct; he wants to do things with other people; he wants activity in friendship; and thus the conception of the game, and especially the team game, is born. But man has also the instinct of competition, and in the game the instinct of competition is harmlessly and healthily satisfied. Thus pleasure fills an essential gap in the life of man. Without it a man's personality cannot be fully developed.

ii. Within this general background pleasure has at least two definite aims and uses. *Pleasure relaxes the mind.* The mind can become tired just as the body can become tired. It comes to a stage when it works slowly and laboriously like a machine running down. It comes to a time when it works inefficiently, and when it makes mistakes. Anyone who uses a typewriter knows that the tireder he gets the more typing errors he makes and that there comes a time when the only sensible thing is to stop. In industry there tends to be, when work is really hard, a decreasing efficiency from Monday to Friday. The relaxation of the mind is essential.

John Cassian tells a famous story about the apostle John. John was one day stroking a tame partridge. Just then a famous philosopher came to visit him, and the philosopher was dressed as a hunter, for he was going on to hunt after he had visited John. He was astonished to find so famous a man as John playing with a tame bird, and he said so. He said he would never have expected to find John doing a thing like that. 'What is that you are carrying in your hand?' John said. 'A bow,' said the philosopher. 'Do you,' asked John, 'carry it always and everywhere bent, taut and at full stretch?' 'No, indeed,' said the philosopher. 'If I kept it at full stretch all the time, it would soon lose its elasticity; and the arrows would fly neither true nor straight nor fast.' John answered that it is exactly the same with the human mind. Unless there are times when it is relaxed, the mind cannot follow its search for truth as it ought. 'The bow that is always bent will soon cease to shoot straight.' And the mind which is always at full stretch will soon cease to be efficient.

Everyone needs some relaxation. He may find it doing nothing; he may find it in a hobby; he may find it in a game; he may find it in music; he may find it in reading a detective novel; he may find it by going fishing or by spending an hour with his stamp collection or with his model railway. When a man is engaged on these things at the right time, he is far from wasting his time. He is recharging the energies of his mind.

iii. Pleasure refreshes the body. Two of the great masters of the spiritual life have pointed out that sometimes, when a man feels that there is something spiritually wrong with him, the trouble is physical and not spiritual at all. Philip Doddridge has a sermon on 'Spiritual Dryness' in which he writes:

> Give me leave to offer you some plain advice in regard to it . . . And here I would first advise you most carefully to enquire whether your present distress does really arise from causes which are truly spiritual? Or whether it does not rather have its foundations in some disorder of body or in the circumstances of life in which you are providentially placed, which may break your spirits and deject your mind? . . . The state of the blood is often such as necessarily to suggest gloomy ideas even in dreams, and to indispose the soul for taking pleasure in anything; and, when it is so, why should it be imagined to proceed from any peculiar divine displeasure, if it does not find its usual delight in religion? . . . When this is the case, the help of the physician is to be sought rather than that of the divine, or, at least, by all means together with it; and medicine, diet, exercise and air may in a few weeks effect that which the strongest reasonings, the most pathetic exhortation or consolations, might for many months have attempted in vain.

The advice of Doddridge is plain—if you think that there is something wrong with your mind and your soul, check on your body first. Richard Baxter has a sermon 'Praise and Meditation' in which he writes:

> I advise thee, as a further help to this heavenly life, not to neglect the care of thy bodily health. Thy body is an useful servant, if thou give it its due, and no more than its due; but it is a most devouring tyrant, if thou suffer it to have what it unreasonably desires; and it is as a blunted knife, if thou unjustly deny it what is necessary to its support . . . There are a few who much hinder their heavenly joy by denying the body its necessaries, and so making it unable to serve them; if such wronged their flesh only, it would be no great matter; but they wrong their souls also; as he that spoils the house injures the inhabitants. When the body is sick and the spirits languish, how heavily do we move in the thoughts and joys of heaven!

So two of the great masters of the spiritual life lay it down that the surest way to injure the spiritual life is to neglect the body. The truth is that many a man might work better if he played more. Pleasure is that which relaxes the mind and refreshes the body, and it is no credit to a man, only a sign of grave unwisdom, if he says that he has no time for it.

In his 1520 manifesto, *Concerning Christian Liberty*, Luther writes:

> It is the part of a Christian to take care of his own body for the very purpose that, by its soundness and well-being, he may be enabled to labour, and to acquire and preserve property, for the aid of those who are in want, that thus the stronger member may serve the weaker member, and we may be the children of God, thoughtful and busy one for another, bearing one another's burdens, and so fulfilling the law of Christ.

It is as if Luther said that, if not for his own sake, then for the sake of others and of the service that he must render them as a Christian man, a Christian ought to care for his body.

But general principles have always to be tested by particular applications. There are then certain pleasures which we must look at in the light of the Christian ethic. We choose three, because they are built into modern society.

1. There is, first, gambling. There has never been an age which did not gamble, for gambling seems little short of a human instinct. But the figures for the present time are staggering. Something like £1,000,000,000 a year changes hands in betting transactions. In 1965 the various figures were as follows: On greyhound racing bets amounted to £110,000,000; on football pools, £73,000,000; on horse-racing, £615,000,000; on fixed odds football betting, £65,000,000; on bingo, £35,000,000. There were then 15,500 betting shops. 12,000,000 people engage in the football pools every week. (It is interesting to note that, when the government has taken its tax, and when expenses have been met, about 8s. in the £1 remains for distribution in winning dividends.) There were 12,363 bingo halls, and the membership of the bingo clubs totalled more than 14,250,000. The charge for taking part in bingo, apart altogether from stake money and club membership money, amounted to £11,700,000. These are staggering figures (cf. R. H. Fuller and B. K. Rice, *Christianity and the Affluent Society*, pp. 80, 81). When we consider this whole matter, there are two facts in the general background at which we must look.

(a) The most universal form of gambling is football pools. These pools began thirty or forty years ago. That is to say, they began at the time when unemployment was always a threat and when life for the working man was permanently insecure. In those days in the early and middle thirties such gambling did not arise from anything like a gambling fever. It arose from a very simple and a very pathetic dream of some kind of security on the part of the working man. If only he had enough to meet that threat of the loss of his work without sheer terror. He was living always on the edge of the precipice of unemployment, and it was here he saw his way of escape. That is not so now. In the age of the affluent society, the desire is not for subsistence; it is for luxury—which is a very different thing. The element of pathos is no longer there.

(b) In the present social structure there is another factor. It is the simple fact that there is hardly any way of becoming really rich other than by one of these immense wins which are publicised. Under the present tax structure, if a man had an income of £24,000 a year, he would pay £18,000 in income tax; if he had an income of £100,000 a year, £83,000 of it would be consumed in tax. The only way to get wealth and to get it quickly, and to get it and keep it, is by a big pools or betting win.

These factors help to build gambling into the social background of the time. There is in the Bible no definite instruction about gambling; we cannot quote this or that text; we have to approach the matter from first principles.

i. The gambler had better begin by facing the fact that all the chances are against him. His chances of losing are far greater than his chances of winning, and his chances of a really big win are very slim indeed.

ii. There are few activities which gain such a grip of a man. It is a common saying of wives that they would rather that their husbands drank than that they gambled. Gambling can become a fever which can leave a man penniless. To go into a casino and to watch professional gamblers at work is a grim experience. There is a bleak and deadly silence and a look on faces which have nothing remotely to do with what we would ordinarily call pleasure.

iii. It is not irrelevant to remember the effect of gambling on sport. Horses and dogs can be doped; more rarely, players can be bribed. Gambling is often allied to crime.

iv. From the point of view of the Christian ethic, the case against gambling can be based on two things.

(a) Basically, gambling is an effort to gain money without working. It is an attempt to become wealthy with no contribution whatever to the common good. The gambler produces nothing and hopes to gain much. Gambling is a deliberate attempt to bypass the essential social principle that reward should go to productive labour. Gambling literally attempts to get money for nothing.

(b) In gambling all winning is based on someone else's losing. In order that one should win another must lose. One person's good fortune is based on another person's ill fortune. One man's winnings are paid out of another man's losses, losses that all too often the loser can ill afford.

It may be argued that the harmless 'flutter' which a man can well afford, that the raffle, the sweepstake and so on can do no harm. They are the very things which can start a man on a way of excitement which can end in very serious harm. It would be well that the Christian and the church should have nothing whatever to do with gambling, which has reached the proportion of a social menace.

2. There is drug-taking. Drug-taking may well be the supreme problem of the present generation.

i. We live in a drug-conscious society. We live a pill-dominated life. People expect to be supplied with a tranquilliser which will pacify them, or a stimulant which will rouse them; and we can even have the bizarre situation of one man at the same time being supplied with a tranquilliser to soothe him, and a stimulant to remove the depression which the tranquilliser caused. No one doubts there is a legitimate and beneficial use of these things. But the root trouble about them is that they are fundamentally a deliberate evasion. They seldom cure; all they do is to hide or mask the symptoms under a cloak of synthetic calm. They are basically and fundamentally an attempt to escape from reality—and the trouble is that reality has a way of catching up with us. No drug on earth can permanently tranquillise a man into peace or stimulate him into action. Their action is temporary; they leave the man unchanged—and there lies the problem. They are an attempt to solve a problem by running away from it.

ii. Serious as that problem is, it is much less serious than the problem of the dangerous drugs. The trouble about these drugs is that they do provide an experience which can be in itself a thrill in the initial stages. Young people think it clever to experiment. There are dope peddlers who cash in on the situation, and surely no hell can be too grim for people who grow wealthy by ruining others body and soul. Let us make no mistake about it. The way to the hard and deadly drugs is through the drugs which are allegedly less harmful. As I write this, there is an article in today's *Scotsman* in which a man's story is told. He began with cannabis offered to him in the bar of a public house; he went on to the amphetamines and to methadrine; he proceeded to heroin and to intravenously injected barbiturates; he ended up a morphine addict. His best friend is a victim, assured of death, of drugs because of 'the slow suicide of the hard drugs', and he would never have got to that stage of the ruin of body and soul if he had not started by experimenting with cannabis. No man in his senses can experiment for a thrill with that which can end by being lethal in the most terrible way.

The Christian ethic must be set against this. Certainly freedom is important, but freedom does not include giving people freedom to destroy themselves and giving people freedom to peddle death.

3. We come now to the third of the pleasures characteristic of our present society, the pleasure of drink, of alcohol. This is by far the commonest pleasure, and by far the most controversial. To take only one form of drinking, in one year the production of beer was 29,500,000 barrels, and the amount drunk was 1,032,000,000 gallons. In the ten years between 1955 and 1965 the convictions in the police courts for drunkenness increased by 60 per cent. There are at least 400,000 alcoholics in Britain, of whom one in every five is a woman. In the case of gambling and drug-taking, the actual evidence from scripture is scanty and meagre; in the case of drink it is plentiful and abundant, but by no means consistent. Let us

begin by setting out the scriptural evidence, and let us begin with the Old Testament.

i. For the Old Testament people the staple articles of diet were corn and wine and oil. To talk of corn and wine and oil was for them what talking of bread and butter is to us. The question of abstinence from wine did not arise. In the time of famine even the children call to their mothers: 'Where is the bread and wine?' (Lamentations 2.12). Whenever the people of Palestine wished to talk of their basic food, it was bread and wine of which they spoke (Genesis 27.37; 1 Samuel 16.20; 25.18; 2 Samuel 16.1; 1 Chronicles 12.40; 2 Chronicles 2.10,15; Nehemiah 5.11,18; 10.37,39; 13.5,12; Job 1.13; Jeremiah 40.10,12). It is well to remember that they drank wine in the proportion of two parts of wine to three of water.

ii. It was a sign of the punishment of God when the bread and wine failed. This is what happens when the nation disobeys God and goes its own way (Deuteronomy 28.39; Isaiah 16.10; 24.9). In the day of punishment, when joy is in its twilight and gladness is banished, 'there is an outcry in the streets for lack of wine' (Isaiah 24.7,11). In the blessed days the invitation is to come and buy milk and wine (Isaiah 55.1). It is God who gives the corn, the wine and the oil, and it is God who can withhold them (Deuteronomy 28.51; Hosea 2.9; Haggai 1.11).

iii. The tragedy is when a man labours and then is never allowed to enjoy his wine and oil (Hosea 9.2; Joel 1.10). The definition of peace and prosperity is when a man works in his own vineyard and enjoys the fruits of it (Amos 5.11; Micah 6.15; Zephaniah 1.13).

iv. The corn, the wine and the oil are the gift of God. 'May God give you plenty of corn and wine and oil,' is Isaac's blessing (Genesis 27.28). The promised land is a land of grain and wine (Deuteronomy 33.28; Isaiah 36.17). 'Honour the Lord and your vats will be bursting with wine' (Proverbs 5.10; Deuteronomy 7.13). It is the fault of Israel that she does not see that it is God who gives the corn, the wine and the oil (Isaiah 65.8).

There is no doubt that in the Old Testament the corn, the wine and the oil are the gifts of God. Certainly, they may be sinfully misused; certainly, they have their dangers; but they are freely to be enjoyed.

There is another side of the picture. Drunkenness was to blame for the shame of Noah (Genesis 9.21-24); the incest of Lot (Genesis 19.20-38); it played its part in the murder of Uriah (2 Samuel 11.13) and of Ammon (2 Samuel 13.23-29). It was a law for the priests: 'Do not drink wine or strong drink when you go into the tent of the meeting' (Leviticus 10.9; Ezekiel 44.21). The rebellious son who is a glutton and a drunkard is guilty of a sin punishable by death (Deuteronomy 21.20). Part of the Nazirite vow was temporary abstinence from wine (Numbers 6.3; Amos 2.12) Jeremiah tells of the Rechabites who were under a permanent vow of abstinence (Jeremiah 35). It is exactly this double view which presents us with our problem.

i. There are many passages in the Old Testament where the excellence of wine is praised and its use commended. It was a regular part of the equipment of the temple, although not for the priests on duty (1 Chronicles 9.29). It was part of the first-fruits to which the Levites were entitled (Deuteronomy 18.4). It was part of the tithes which were to be 'eaten before the Lord' (Deuteronomy 14.22-27). 'Wine or strong drink or whatever your appetite craves . . . you shall eat before the Lord and rejoice.' Wine was a regular part of the daily sacrifice (Exodus 29.40). Wine was a standard part of the sacrificial system (Numbers 15.5-10; 28.7-14).

Wine is the symbol of that which is best and most joyous. Only love is better than wine (Song of Solomon 1.2,4; 4.10; 7.9). Wine is part of Wisdom's feast (Proverbs 9.2,5). Wine cheers gods and men (Judges 9.13). God gave it to gladden the heart of man (Psalm 104.15). It is to be given to those who faint in the wilderness (2 Samuel 16.2). Wine in plenty was to be a picture of the golden age to come. 'They shall plant vineyards and drink their wine' (Amos 9.14; Joel 2.24; 3.18;

Isaiah 25.6; 62.8). 'They shall be radiant over the goodness of the Lord, over the grain, the wine and the oil' (Jeremiah 31.12). 'Go your way,' says the Preacher. 'Eat your bread with enjoyment, and drink your wine with a merry heart, for God has already approved what you do.' 'Bread is made for laughter and wine gladdens life, and [an odd sentiment to find in Scripture!] money answers everything' (Ecclesiastes 9.7; 10.19).

The Old Testament has much to say about the joy and the delight of the God-given wine.

ii. But there is another side in the Old Testament. The Old Testament was acutely aware of the danger of wine. Very naturally the prudent Wisdom literature emphasises this. 'Wine is a mocker, strong drink a brawler; and whoever is led astray by it is not wise' (Proverbs 20.1). 'He who loves wine and oil will not be rich' (Proverbs 21.17). 'The drunkard and the glutton will come to poverty' (Proverbs 21.17; 23.20). There are two long passages in Proverbs which must be quoted in full:

> *Who has woe? Who has sorrow?*
> *Who has strife? Who has complaining?*
> *Who has wounds without cause?*
> *Who has redness of eyes?*
> *Those who tarry long over wine,*
> *those who go to try mixed wine.*
> *Do not look at wine when it is red,*
> *when it sparkles in the cup,*
> *and goes down smoothly.*
> *At last it bites like a serpent,*
> *and stings like an adder.*
> *Your eyes will see strange things,*
> *and your mind utter perverse things.*
> *You will be like one who lies down in the midst of the sea,*
> *like one who lies on the top of a mast.*

'They struck me,' you will say, 'but I was not hurt;
  they beat me but I did not feel it.
When shall I awake?
  I will seek another drink' (Proverbs 23.29-35).

It is not for kings, O Lemuel,
  it is not for kings to drink wine,
  or for rulers to desire strong drink;
lest they drink and forget what has been decreed,
  and pervert the rights of all the afflicted.
Give strong drink to him who is perishing,
  and wine to those in bitter distress;
let them drink and forget their poverty,
  and remember their misery no more (Proverbs 31.4-7).

It is only to be expected that the prophets with their strong ethical bent would be very much aware of the dangers of wine. 'Wine and new wine,' says Hosea, 'will take away the understanding' (Hosea 4.11). 'Princes become sick with the heat of wine' (Hosea 7.5). 'Wine is treacherous' (Habakkuk 2.5).

To the sin of drunkenness the prophets are merciless. 'Woe to the proud crown of the drunkards of Ephraim,' says Isaiah (Isaiah 28.1). 'They also reel with wine, and stagger with strong drink; the priest and the prophet reel with strong drink; they are confused with wine; they stagger with strong drink; they err in vision; they stumble in giving judgment. For all tables are full of vomit; no place is without filthiness' (Isaiah 28.7,8). 'Woe to them who rise early in the morning that they may run after strong drink, who tarry late in the evening till wine inflames them' (Isaiah 5.11). 'Woe to those who are heroes at drinking wine, and valiant men in mixing strong drink, who acquit the guilty for a bribe, and deprive the innocent of his right' (Isaiah 5.22). Isaiah rebukes those who say: 'Let us eat and drink for tomorrow we die.' 'Come, let us get wine. Let us fill ourselves with strong drink, for tomorrow will be like today, great beyond measure' (Isaiah 22.13; 56.12).

There then is the Old Testament evidence. To put it briefly—the Old Testament looks on wine as one of the good gifts of God; it nowhere demands total abstinence from it; but there is no book which is more intensely aware of its dangers, and which more unsparingly condemns its misuse.

Finally, we turn to the evidence of the New Testament. In the New Testament the material is not so extensive, but we meet with the same general attitude. Jesus himself was not a total abstainer; they could slanderously call him a glutton and a drunkard (Matthew 11.19; Luke 7.34). The miracle of Cana of Galilee shows Jesus willing to share in the simple joys of a wedding-feast (John 2.1-11). Paul can send advice to Timothy: 'No longer drink only water, but use a little wine for the sake of your stomach and your frequent ailments' (1 Timothy 5.23).

But the voice of warning is there. The bad servant in the parable eats and drinks with the drunken (Matthew 24.49). 'Do not get drunk with wine,' says Paul, 'for that is debauchery' (Ephesians 5.18). When the New Testament lists sins, sins in which the Christian must have no part, revelry, drunkenness, carousing regularly appear among the forbidden things (Romans 13.13; 1 Corinthians 6.10; Galatians 5.21). There are even times when drunken conduct invades the church and its Love Feasts (1 Corinthians 11.21; 2 Peter 2.13), and there are those who have to be warned against drunkenness at night (1 Thessalonians 5.7). In particular those who hold office in the church are warned against any excess. There must be no association with a drunkard (1 Corinthians 5.11). The older women are not to be addicted to drink (Titus 2.3). The deacons are not to be slaves to wine, and the bishop is not to be a drunkard (1 Timothy 3.8; 3.3; Titus 1.7).

One passage must have special treatment. The saying in Colossians 2.21 is often used as evidence for total abstinence—'Do not handle; do not taste; do not touch.' It is precisely the reverse. In the passage Paul is dealing with those who are preaching a false asceticism, and who are trying to introduce new food laws which will prohibit people from eating this, that, and the next thing. And this saying is the saying of the *heretics*, who are trying to mislead the people. It is the heretics and the misguided and misleading teachers who say, 'Do not handle; do not taste; do not touch,' and this the Revised Standard Version makes quite clear by putting the sentence into quotation marks, in order to show that it is a quotation from the false teaching of the heretical teachers. This sentence tells us, not what to do, but what not to do.

This, then, is the New Testament evidence. Once again there is nowhere any demand for total abstinence, neither in the words nor in the example of Jesus or of his followers, but there is a strong warning against the misuse and the danger of drink. In this case we have no rule and regulation on which to fall back. We must work out our own conclusion.

Before we begin to work out a view of this question of total abstinence or of the Christian attitude to the use of alcohol, we may note that this is a comparatively new question. We have already seen that neither in the Old Testament nor in the New Testament did the demand arise. Nor were the reformers against the use of alcohol. Luther enjoyed his wine and his beer. When he was hidden away in the castle of the Wartburg, he wrote to Spalatin: 'As for me, I sit here all day long, at ease with my wine. I am reading the Bible in Greek and Hebrew.' John Kessler tells how he and another Swiss student met Luther in an inn, not at first aware that it was Luther. Luther paid for their dinner. Kessler tells the charming story: 'Then he (Luther) took a tall glass of beer and said in the manner of the country, "Now you two Swiss, let us drink together a friendly drink, for our evening Grace." But as I went to take the glass from him, he changed his mind and said, "You aren't used to our outlandish beer; come, drink wine instead".' Luther says in a 1522 Wittenberg sermon that the work that was in progress was none of his doing; it was the work of the Word of God. 'I simply taught, preached and wrote God's word; otherwise I did nothing. And while I slept (cf. Mark 4.26-29), or drank Wittenberg beer with my friends Philip (Melanchthon) and (Nicholas von) Amsdorf, the Word so greatly weakened the Papacy that no prince or emperor ever inflicted such losses upon it. I did nothing; the Word did everything.' It did not occur to Luther to abstain from alcohol. Nor did it strike the early Methodists. Charles Wesley writes to his wife Sally that 'a glass of wine helps him in his indispositions. And he always carries his own Madeira with him on his journeys' (Frederick C. Gill, *Charles Wesley, the first Methodist*, p. 174). When George Whitefield set off for America, amidst a host of other stores he took with him 'a firkin of butter, a Cheshire cheese, a Gloucestershire cheese, one hundred lemons, two hogsheads of fine white wine, three barrels of raisins' (Arnold Dallimore, *George Whitefield*, p. 144). The practice of Thomas Chalmers of Disruption fame is interesting. His resolution was 'not to take more than three glasses of wine at a sitting'. Dr McDonald of Ferintish was so famous a preacher that he was known as the Apostle of the North. Cunningham the historian tells us of him: 'Twelve or fifteen glasses of whisky daily rejoiced his heart and simply produced a pleasant glow upon his countenance' (Ian Henderson, *Scotland: Kirk and People*, pp. 100, 101). From another source we learn that in September 1824 in Glasgow, Thomas Chalmers' cellar was composed of: 71 bottles of Madeira; 41 of port; 14 of sherry; 22 of Teneriffe; 10 of claret; and 44 of whisky.

On the other hand, William Booth was inflexibly opposed to the use of alcohol. In the conditions of his day he could not use it. Richard Collier describes the London scene: 'London's 100,000 pubs, laid end to end, would have stretched a full thirty miles. In East London alone, the heart of Booth's territory, every fifth shop was a gin-shop; most kept special steps to help even tiny mites reach the counter. The pubs featured penny glasses of gin for children; too often child alcoholics needed the stomach-pump. Children less than five years old knew the raging agonies of delirium tremens or died from cirrhosis of the liver. Others trudged through the Sunday streets bringing yet more gin to parents who lay drunk and fully clothed in bed, vomiting on the floor. These were the by-products of a £100 million a year trade, whose worst victims slept on heaps of soot beneath the arches of Blackfriars Bridge, living only for the next glass' (Richard Collier, *The General next to God*, p. 53). On practical grounds, Booth was unalterably opposed to the use of alcohol, and his Salvationists were and are pledged to total abstinence.

i. The prevalence of the use of alcohol in all grades of society is ample proof of its attraction. It makes entertaining easy; it relaxes tensions and eases the atmosphere of a social occasion. There is the occasional medical use of it, of which even Paul's advice to Timothy is an example. We need not argue about the attraction; it is there.

ii. But in addition to the attraction there are obvious dangers.

(a) There is the fact that the effect of alcohol on a man is quite unpredictable. One man may be able to take it in even large quantities with no visible ill effect; another man may be liable to become drunk on the smallest quantity; another man may have that built into his composition which makes him an alcoholic, and he may be such that any use of alcohol will have the most disastrous effects. None of these effects can be predicted in advance. Only experiment shows how a man will react, and it can be argued that the experiment carries with it such a risk that it is unwise to make it.

(b) There is the danger of excess. It is quite true that the danger of excess arises with any pleasure, and that scripture warns against gluttony just as strongly as it warns against drunkenness. But drunkenness is a specially ugly thing in a drunken person, and a specially unhappy thing for those with whom he lives and who share his life and home.

(c) With alcohol there arises the question of addiction. One of the characteristics of alcohol is that, as time goes on, it requires an ever-increasing amount of it to produce the same effect. What in the beginning was a pleasure becomes in the end an overmastering desire. The habit is formed, and the habit is desperately hard to break. A man will do well to think whether it is wise to begin something to which he may well end by becoming a slave.

(d) There is the matter of expense. Drinking is nowadays one of the most expensive pleasures; and a man may well find himself spending money on a luxury which should have been kept for the necessities.

(e) There are the general effects of alcohol. It can impair a man's efficiency and dull his brain. It can slow down his reflexes and his reactions, which is why the law is so stern to those who drive a motor car under its influence. It can slur a man's speech. But it has one effect which is more serious in its own way than any of the others. Alcohol does not only relax tensions; it also relaxes a man's self-control and renders him liable to do and to say things which in his sober senses he would not do or say. In particular, it loosens a person's moral control, and sexual immorality and alcohol very often have a very close connection. Alcohol, especially if it is used to excess, can make a man behave in ways in which he would not ordinarily behave. There is therefore in alcohol an inbuilt danger.

All this is true, but all this does not settle the matter. All that has been said could be said of almost any pleasure that has got out of control. There are many drugs which are at one and the same time dangerous drugs and useful drugs. There are many habits which are useful in moderation but harmful in excess. If the man who takes alcohol risks danger to his stomach and to his liver, the man who smokes risks danger to his lungs, and the man who consistently eats too much and moves too little risks the stomach ulcer and the thrombosis. The physical danger argument is not a good argument, for a man might answer quite simply that he is aware of the danger and that he chooses to face it.

In the last analysis the only argument against the misuse of

alcohol is the argument from responsibility for our brother-
man. We have here the old tension between freedom and
responsibility. Paul is quite clear that no man has any right
to lay down what any other man may eat or drink (Colossians
2.21). The classic passage is in Romans 14.1-8. There Paul
refuses to arbitrate between those who hold different ideas of
what it is right to do. If a man holds that what he does is as
far as he is concerned right in the sight of God, then no one
can criticise. On the other hand, there is the responsibility
never to cause a brother to stumble or fall by what we eat or
drink (1 Corinthians 8.13; Romans 14.20,21). The liberty of
the strong must never become a stumbling block to the weak
(1 Corinthians 8.9). Certainly, all things are lawful, but all
things are not helpful, and nothing must be allowed to master
us (1 Corinthians 6.12).

But even this does not free us from making our own personal
choice. The biblical writers, Paul, Jesus himself knew the
dangers of drink as well as we do, for every age has known
what drunkenness means, and yet, while they unhesitatingly
condemned excess, they never demanded total abstention. The
decision is left to us, and on soul and conscience we must
make it, and some will decide one way and some another—
and they have liberty to do so.

The one thing to avoid is a censorious self-righteousness.
W. M. Macgregor, in *The Making of a Preacher*, says: 'Nearly
sixty years ago I knew a crusty, ill-tempered woman, who
lived alone in one very dismal room, with no apparent means
of support but her parish allowance and occasional charity.
Her neighbours resented her caustic tongue, so her solitude
was seldom invaded, but at vague intervals she started on a
pilgrimage among old acquaintances, from each of whom she
exacted a contribution of at least one penny, and on the proceeds of the tour she got satisfactorily drunk. The deliberation
of what she did gave it an ugly look, and she was appealed
to and denounced as peculiarly a sinner, but only once, as I
was told, did she retort: "Wad ye grudge me my one chance

141

o' getting clean out o' the Pans wi' a sup of whisky?" ' Her one chance of escape from the Pans, the grim slum in which she lived, was occasionally to drink.

Whatever else we say, and whatever stand we adopt, those of us who have comfortable and happy homes should not be too hard on the person whose only club is the pub; those of us who have many friends should not be too hard on the lonely one who turns to the public house for company; those of us who have no fears and tensions should not be too hard on the person who seeks to relax with drink.

We can do no more than leave the verdict in suspense for each man to make his own decision. We are not the keeper of any man's conscience. But let the man who emerges with one verdict not condemn the man who emerges with another.

In life there must be pleasure, and the ideal pleasure is that which is harmless to the person who indulges in it and to all other people, which brings help to him who practises it and happiness to others.

CHAPTER SEVEN

The Christian and his Money

It will be well to look at the situation against which we are discussing the Christian and his money. I am indebted for many of the facts I shall quote in the earlier part of this discussion to *Christianity and the Affluent Society*, by Reginald H. Fuller and Brian K. Rice (pp. 63-149). That book was published in 1966; its statistics therefore come from 1965, but they are the statistics of a situation which has not altered, except to become intensified. So then let us look at the present situation.

i. We are living in what has been called the affluent society. F. R. Barry in his book *Christian Ethics and Secular Society* (p. 267) does not deny that poverty still exists, but he says that for the great majority of Christians 'the call is now to the sanctification of wealth'. Brian K. Rice (*op. cit.*, p. 170) writes: 'Affluence in the hands of fallen man is a double-edged blessing and the source of much evil.' Affluence, wealth, are the key-words.

The Board of Trade prepares the cost of living index, and that index is based on the price of things which may be deemed as part of the equipment of an ordinary household. In 1900 neither butter nor electricity was included in that list. In 1962 washing-machines and television sets appeared. In 1938 it took sixty-five weeks' wages to buy a motor car; it now takes thirty-six and a half weeks' wages. Two homes out of every five have a car, and one in ten have more than one car. The national hire purchase debt in 1965 was £1,378,000,000, £21 16s. for every man, woman and child in the country.

There are about fourteen million combined television and sound licences, and another three million licences for sound only. In the ten years before 1965 the number of homes with refrigerators rose from 8.1 per cent to 41 per cent. In 1965 five million people holidayed abroad at a cost of £200,000,000 and about a quarter of them had a second holiday at home. Even their holiday photographs cost £70,000,000! The country spends about £1,330,000,000 a year on tobacco, of which £1,000,000,000 goes in tax. Eighty-six per cent of the homes in the country have television. (And perhaps two million sets have never had a licence paid for their use.) £100,000,000 a year is spent on toiletries and cosmetics, £40,000,000 on hair preparations, and £70,000,000 on hair-dressing. Every day £2,000,000 is spent on advertising.

That is the kind of society in which we live; that is the meaning of the affluent society.

ii. But there is another side to this society. As Brian K. Rice says that it might be put: 'The things which are flourishing amidst our prosperity are venereal disease, mental disorder, bad debts, juvenile delinquency, drug addiction, strikes, bankruptcy, crime.' Let us look at only a few of the facts.

At any one time there are 200,000 mentally disturbed patients in hospital. In fact, half the people in hospitals are in some form or other mental patients. There are 7,000 suicides a year, and ten times as many people attempt suicide each year. There are probably 500,000 in Britain who have tried to take their own lives. And Britain's suicide rate is comparatively low. In Austria the suicide rate is 24·9 per thousand people; in Denmark, 23·5; in Finland, 22·9; in Switzerland, 22·6; in Sweden, 21·1; in Britain 12·3. Suicides from overdoses of drugs increased from 787 to 1,038 in one year. In the last fifteen years suicides by use of the barbiturate drugs have increased ten times over, and attempted suicides by use of the barbiturates amount to 8,000-10,000 a year.

At any moment there are 30,000 people in gaol. Before the

war there were 3,000 crimes of personal violence per year; now there are more than 20,000.

In spite of the affluent society there are 1,500,000 households with no indoor lavatory; 3,640,000 without a fixed inside bath; three million with no hot water tap; and 246,000 without even a cold water tap. Two thousand people sleep rough in London every night.

Side by side with the affluence there are terrible things, and there is poverty and bad housing, which lcok all the worse for their comparison with the general affluence.

iii. There is another paradox. In one sense this situation is one with the greatest possible opportunities. There is a health service with the best attention available to all. There is now no reason why any young person with the necessary ability should not receive a university education. There are almost limitless possibilities of increased production, with higher wages, more things to possess, increased leisure. In one sense to look ahead is a dazzling prospect.

iv. But there is another side to this, and for this other side Brian K. Rice supplies certain facts from America which provide very serious food for thought.

The outstanding development in America is the arrival of the computer and of electronic systems. The speed with which this has happened is shown by the fact that in 1958 there were only 450 computers in America. Here is a selection of the things which have happened and are happening.

In America the computer and the electronic systems are putting anything from 40,000 to 70,000 people out of work every week. There are in that very advanced and very wealthy country between thirty million and forty million people living in poverty and squalor 'in slums, migratory labour camps, depressed areas, Indian reservations'. At least thirty million go hungry in America. Why?

A company in Michigan which supplies electricity to 50,000 homes dismissed 300 meter-readers and half its office staff, because customers are now linked to a computer which registers the current used, makes out the account, and addresses the envelope. In a motor-car factory there is a computing machine which can make up the wages of 26,000 employees, differing rates, overtime and everything else, in half an hour. There is a machine which can print a 300-page book in three hours. A government department handling pensions has been able to reduce its staff from 17,000 to 3,000. There is a radio factory in Chicago where by electronic processes 1,000 radio transistor sets can be produced each day, and the whole process is tended by two men—instead of 200 as formerly. There is a bottling plant which can clean, refill, cap and crate 200,000 bottles per day, with a total staff of three men. The New York telephone exchange is twenty storeys high and handles millions of calls a day. The total staff is five, two on duty and three on stand-by. Macey's store experimented with a robot machine which can sell thirty-six different garments, in ten styles and sizes, which accepts coins or notes, and gives change, and which screams if any one tries to feed it with counterfeit money.

What is happening is obvious. Since the war 400,000 coal-miners have lost their jobs; 250,000 steel-workers; 300,000 textile-workers; and the whole process is just beginning.

Brian K. Price quotes a labour leading figure: 'There is no element of blessing in automation. It is rapidly becoming a real curse to society, and it could bring us to a national catastrophe.' What happens—it is Mr Price's question—when man is unnecessary? It has already been suggested that the day will come when a married man with one child will be paid one hundred dollars a week to *stay at home*. 'Society must accept,' so it has been said, 'that work as we know it must eventually disappear. Man as a working instrument is heading towards obsolescence.' And the result already is that there is poverty and unemployment in America on a scale almost unknown in Britain.

This is the background of our present situation. We have not yet in this country encountered the full problem. If we are wise enough to do so, we can learn from the experience of others how to face it. But here are the paradoxes of the affluent society in which men make and spend and give and save their money.

Let us then go to the Bible and see what it teaches about wealth and possessions. We begin with the Old Testament, and we find in it an abundance of material.

i. It has been said—and it is as true or as false as most epigrams—that prosperity is the blessing of the Old Testament and adversity of the New Testament. The Old Testament expects to find the good man flourishing and prosperous; the New Testament expects to find him afflicted and in trouble.

It is true that in the Old Testament there is a strong line of thought which does connect prosperity with goodness and adversity with wickedness, just as Job's comforters did. It is indeed very significant that after all his afflictions Job does finish up with renewed and increased prosperity (Job 42.10-17). 'I have been young and now am old,' said the Psalmist, 'yet I have not seen the righteous forsaken, or his children begging bread' (Psalm 37.25). The reward for humility and fear of the Lord is riches and honour and life (Proverbs 30.8,9). The blessing of the Lord makes rich (Proverbs 10.22). Wealth and riches are in the house of the man who fears the Lord (Psalm 112.3). Wisdom has long life in her right hand, and honour and riches in her left. Riches and honour are with her, lasting wealth and prosperity (Proverbs 3.16; 8.18). The Old Testament does connect goodness and prosperity.

ii. In the Old Testament there is a line of thought which sees the way to happiness as having neither too much nor too little. The wise man prays to God: 'Give me neither poverty nor riches, lest I be full and deny thee, and say, "Who is the Lord?", or lest I be poor, and steal and profane the name of my God' (Proverbs 30.8,9). This would be very much in line with the Greek doctrine of the happy medium.

iii. The Old Testament is sure that prosperity is a gift from

147

God, and that no man should forget that it is so. The preacher talks of the man to whom God has given wealth and possessions and the power to enjoy them. 'This,' he says 'is the gift of God' (Ecclesiastes 5.19). And if wealth is the gift of God, a man must use it in stewardship for God.

iv. Wealth does not fall into a man's lap with no effort from him. 'A slack hand causes poverty,' says the wise man, 'but the hand of the diligent makes rich' (Proverbs 10.4). As the Greek Hesiod had it: 'The gods have placed sweat as the price of all good things.'

v. There is a kind of security that wealth can bring. 'A rich man's wealth is his strong city, and like a high wall protecting him' (Proverbs 18.11; 10.15). There are things from which wealth can protect a man. There is an old Scots saying: 'Sorrow is not so sore, when there is a loaf of bread.' To be left alone is always a sore thing, but to be left alone and in destitution is still worse.

vi. But even if there is a kind of security in wealth, there is also an essential inadequacy in it too. 'The righteous man will flourish, but the man who trusts in riches will wither' (Proverbs 11.38). Wealth is no substitute for character and goodness. It is durable riches that wisdom gives (Proverbs 8.18). When it comes to a matter of meeting the judgment of God, riches do not profit; it is righteousness which delivers a man from death (Proverbs 11.4). Even if riches do increase, a man is not to set his heart upon them (Psalm 62.10). There is no permanence about them; riches do not last for ever (Proverbs 27.24). Wealth may be a gift from God, but wealth is not everything.

vii. At best wealth is a secondary good. A good name is to be chosen rather than great riches, and favour is better than silver or gold (Proverbs 22.1). Better a little that the righteous has than the abundance of many wicked (Psalm 37.16). The sleep of the labouring man is sounder than the sleep of the rich (Ecclesiastes 5.12). It is only a short-sighted man who concentrates everything on the search for wealth

(Proverbs 28.22). When a man dies he will carry nothing away (Psalm 49.16). He came naked into the world, and naked he will leave it (Job 1.21). As a man came from his mother's womb, so he will go back again. He takes nothing of his toil that he can carry away in his hand. He has toiled for the wind (Ecclesiastes 5.15,16). A man should be wise enough to cease the struggle for wealth. 'When your eyes light upon it, it is gone; for suddenly it takes to itself wings, flying like an eagle towards heaven' (Proverbs 23.4,5).

He will be a foolish man to give his life to that which he cannot take with him, and to that which he can lose at any moment.

viii. There are occasions when wealth can hinder rather than help. A man can keep riches to his hurt (Ecclesiastes 5.13). There is no profit for the man who gets riches in the wrong way. 'In the midst of his days they will leave him, and at his end he will be a fool' (Jeremiah 17.11). Wealth can make a man careless of God and of his fellow men. How can God know? he will ask. The wicked take their careless ease, but the day of reckoning comes (Psalm 73.12). Some day the righteous will laugh at the man 'who would not make God his refuge and sought refuge in his wealth' (Psalm 52.7).

ix. Undoubtedly wealth gives a man power over his fellow men. 'The rich rules over the poor, and the borrower is the slave of the lender' (Proverbs 22.7). Wealth gives a man a certain popularity. 'The poor is disliked even by his neighbours, but the rich has many friends' (Proverbs 14.20). Wealth can bring with it pride and arrogance, and these are the sins which go before a fall. 'The poor may have to use entreaties, but the rich answers roughly' (Proverbs 28.11). The wise man never glories in his riches, any more than the wise man in his wisdom, or the mighty man in his might (Jeremiah 9.23). The rich man tends to be a man who is full of violence (Micah 6.12). Wealth can do things to a man which make him a far worse man, and to possess it is not a sin, but a danger to character.

x. On at least one occasion in the Old Testament the rich man is synonymous with the wicked man. It is said of the suffering servant that they made his grave with the wicked, and with a rich man in his death (Isaiah 53.9).

The writers of the Old Testament know that wealth is a gift from God, but they also know that it can separate a man from God and from his fellow men. They know that wealth is a good thing for a man to enjoy, but a bad thing for a man to put his trust in, or to give his life to.

We shall gain further light on this, if we look at what the Old Testament has to say about the poor.

The Old Testament uses three words for *poor*. It uses the word *dal* which means poor and weak and even emaciated. It is, for instance, the word that is used of the lean cattle in Pharaoh's dream (Genesis 41.19). The Revised Standard Version usually translates it *poor* (Proverbs 22.9,16,22; Amos 4.1; 5.11; 8.6); but sometimes it translates it *weak* (Psalm 41.1, margin; Psalm 82.3,4). It uses the word *ebion*, which the Revised Standard Version regularly translates *needy* (Job 5.15; Psalm 69.33; 140.12; Proverbs 14.31; Jeremiah 20.13). This word expresses the state of the man who is not only poor, but whose poverty has brought to him oppression and abuse. It uses the word *ani*. This is what we might call the most developed word. It describes the man who is poor, without influence, oppressed. This man has no human help and no human resources; and in such a state his only help is in God, in whom he has put his trust. So it comes to mean the poor and humble man, whose whole and only trust is in God (Psalm 34.6; 40.17; 68.10; 86.1; Proverbs 14.21; Isaiah 66.2). Here there emerges something which is very much a dominant part of the pattern—the fact that the poor man is specially the concern of God.

i. There is laid upon men the special duty of remembering and helping the poor. Both the wise man and the psalmist speak of the happiness of the man who remembers the poor (Psalm 41.1; Proverbs 14.21). It is part of a good man's duty to maintain the rights of the poor and the needy (Proverbs 31.9). The good man does not regard the rich more than the poor (Job 34.19). The command of God is: 'Give justice to the weak and the fatherless; maintain the right of the afflicted and the destitute. Rescue the weak and the needy; deliver them from the hand of the wicked' (Psalm 82.3,4). Only if a king judges the poor with equity will his throne be established for ever (Proverbs 29.14). As the Old Testament sees it, it is an essential part of a good man's duty to remember, to help and to defend the poor.

ii. In the Old Testament there is also consistent condemnation for those who neglect or ill-treat the poor. It is the wicked who persecute the poor (Psalm 10.2). Part of Isaiah's condemnation of the wicked is that the spoil of the poor is in their houses (Isaiah 3.14,15). 'Woe to those who make iniquitous decrees . . . to turn aside the needy from justice, and to rob the poor of my people of their rights' (Isaiah 10.1-2). It is the activity of the wicked 'to ruin the poor with lying words, even when the plea of the needy is right' (Isaiah 32.7). He who oppresses the poor to increase his own wealth will come to nothing else than want (Proverbs 27.6). 'A righteous man knows the rights of the poor, but a wicked man does not understand such knowledge' (Proverbs 29.7).

It has been said that the voice of the prophets is often nothing other than 'a cry for social justice'. The care of the poor is an essential duty laid on the man who wishes to see the world as God meant it to be.

iii. In the Old Testament the care of the poor is laid down, not only as a duty to man, but also as a duty to God. It is something which has to be done, not only for the sake of the poor, but also for the sake of God. Jeremiah says of a good king: 'He judged the cause of the poor and the needy: then it was well. Is not this to know me? says the Lord' (Jeremiah 22.16). The wise man says: 'He who oppresses the poor insults his Maker, but he who is kind to the needy honours him' (Proverbs 14.31). 'He who is kind to the poor lends to the

Lord' (Proverbs 19.17). If a man closes his ear to the cry of the poor, God will close his ear to his cry (Proverbs 21.13). 'Do not rob the poor because he is poor, or crush the afflicted at the gate; for the Lord will plead their cause, and despoil the life of those who despoil them' (Proverbs 22.22,23).

To help the poor is to help God; to be heartless to them is to incur his anger. How could it be otherwise, for to injure the child is always to anger the child's father, and to help the child is always to delight the child's father's heart?

iv. As we would expect from all this, the Old Testament is sure that God cares for the poor in a very special way, and rescues and delivers them. This is a favourite thought in the Psalms. 'The Lord hears the needy' (Psalm 69.33). 'God stands at the right hand of the needy' (Psalm 109.31). 'The needy shall not always be forgotten, and the hope of the poor shall not perish for ever' (Psalm 9.18). 'This poor man cried and the Lord heard him' (Psalm 44.6). God in his kindness provides for the needy (Psalm 68.10). 'God delivers the needy when he calls, the poor and him who has no helper' (Psalm 72.12). 'The Lord executes justice for the needy' (Psalm 140.12). 'He raises up the poor from the dust' (1 Samuel 2.8). 'With righteousness God will give justice to the poor' (Isaiah 11.4).

The poor man is under the care of God. The Old Testament does not despise wealth; it does not deny that there are things that wealth can do. But it will never make wealth the principal good, and it will always insist that to gain wealth wrongly and to use wealth selfishly are both to sin against God.

We now turn to the New Testament, and in particular to the teaching of Jesus.

i. When we study Jesus' teaching about money, the first thing that emerges is that the assumption of New Testament teaching is that the Christian will live an ordinary life, so far as the work and the obligations of life are concerned. It is assumed that he will be doing a job, earning a pay, paying his way and supporting those who are dependent on him. There are those who have withdrawn from the world, and who have taken the vow of poverty, chastity and obedience. At first sight this seems the very essence of Christianity. But here a paradox emerges. If there are people who vow themselves to poverty, who divorce themselves from the ordinary work of this world, and who live on the charity they receive, if they forswear all possessions, it simply means that the rest of the world must keep on working to enable these people to withdraw from the world and to supply the charity on which they live. If everyone withdrew, and if everyone forswore all earthly possessions, then the whole structure of society would collapse, and, if no one had anything, there would be no one to give anyone anything, and all charity would necessarily come to an end. So we have the odd situation that it is necessary for the 'ordinary' Christians to keep on working in order to make it possible for the 'super' Christians to withdraw from the world. This is not the Christian way. New Testament teaching involves the assumption that the Christian is living a normal life, doing the world's work, and accepting the world's obligations.

This is what Jesus did. The first thirty years of his life were spent in Nazareth (Luke 3.23), where he was well known as the village carpenter (Mark 6.3). He accepted the normal duty of paying taxes, both to the government (Matthew 22.15-22) and to the Temple (Matthew 17.24-27). He and his friends had their own store of money, and it was the task of Judas Iscariot to look after it. When it was a question of feeding the crowds, Philip's first reaction was that the food would have to be paid for (John 6.7). The whole implication is that Jesus and his friends accepted their normal obligations and paid their way.

ii. Exactly the same was true of Paul. He was a qualified tradesman (Acts 18.3) and it was always his claim that, wherever he stayed, he was a burden on no one, because he was self-supporting (1 Corinthians 4.12; 1 Thessalonians 2.9; 2 Thessalonians 3.7,8; Acts 20.34). He earned his money, supported himself, and paid his debts with his own work—and he wanted it that way.

iii. Nevertheless the New Testament is clear about the danger of riches. The New Testament never says that it is a sin to possess money, but it does say that it is a grave danger. 'Woe to you that are rich,' Jesus said, as Luke has it. 'Woe to you that are full now' (Luke 6.24,25). In the story of the rich young ruler (Matthew 19.16-30; Mark 10.17-31; Luke 18.18-30), a story to which we shall return, Jesus warns men that it is desperately difficult for a rich man to get into the kingdom of God. It is not money itself, but the love of money that is the root of all evils (1 Timothy 6.10). The danger is always there.

iv. The danger that a man can become too fond of money can even enter the church. The bishops and the deacons are both warned that they must not be greedy for gain (1 Timothy 3.3,8; Titus 1.7). Those who tend the flock are warned that they must not do so for shameful gain (1 Peter 5.2). There are those in the Christian fellowship who are there to exploit their fellow Christians (2 Peter 2.3). The writer to the Hebrews writes: 'Keep life free from the love of money' (Hebrews 13.5). The attraction of money is something from which the Christian was not, and is not, immune. The sin of covetousness was something of which the New Testament was very much aware (Mark 7.12; Luke 12.15; Romans 1.29; 2 Corinthians 9.5; Ephesians 5.3; Colossians 3.5; 1 Timothy 2.5; 2 Peter 2.3). *Pleonexia*, the Greek word for covetousness, means *the desire to have more*, and that is a desire which is deeply rooted in human nature.

v. There was nothing of inverted snobbery in the attitude of Jesus to wealth. He did not glorify poverty as such. He had friends in every walk of life. James and John came from a family who were well enough off to own their own fishing-boat and to employ hired servants (Mark 1.19,20). Nicodemus brought spices which must have cost a very large sum of money for the anointing of Jesus' body (John 19.39).

Zacchaeus was a wealthy man, and he was not called upon entirely to divest himself of his belongings (Luke 19.1-10). There were certain women who followed Jesus, and who cared for his needs, and of them Joanna, the wife of Chuza, Herod's steward, certainly must have belonged to the upper and the wealthy classes (Luke 8.3). Even if we insist on the dangers of riches, we cannot fly to the other extreme, and make poverty itself a virtue.

vi. One of the dangers of riches, as the New Testament sees it, is that they may beget arrogance in their possessor, and subservient snobbery in those who come into contact with him. In the Pastoral Letters Timothy is instructed to charge the rich in this world's goods not to be haughty (1 Timothy 6.17). James draws the picture of the rich man arriving in the Christian congregation and being treated with a servile snobbery at the expense of the poor (James 2.1-7). And he condemns the rich man who lives in luxury while his employees remain unpaid (James 5.1-6). The New Testament is well aware of the attitude of mind which riches can produce, both in the mind of the man who has them and in the minds of the people who encounter them.

vii. The New Testament is sure that riches are a bad thing in which to put our trust; they are a very insecure foundation for life.

(a) A man has to learn that the value of his life cannot be assessed by the size of his bank balance. The rich man in the parable (Luke 12.13-21) thought that he had enough laid by to enable him to enjoy life for many years to come, but that very night, when he was making his future plans, God required his soul from him, and all the material things of which he had been so proud became a sheer irrelevance. A man cannot take his material possessions to heaven along with him.

(b) Riches are a diminishing asset. The moth and rust can damage them, and the thief can steal them (Matthew 6.19-21). They are no more permanent than the flower which blossoms and fades (James 1.10,11). It has been said that there are people who know 'the price of everything and the value of nothing'. It is when he is confronted with eternity that a man sees the true value of things, and he is a foolish man who puts his confidence in things so easily lost and so quick to deteriorate.

(c) The desire for riches can blind a man to the higher things. 'The cares of this world and delight in riches' are like the fast-growing weeds that choke the life out of the seed (Matthew 13.22; Mark 4.9; Luke 8.14). As William Lillie says in his *Studies in Christian Ethics*: 'The pursuit of money takes the place of the worship of God.' 'No man', said Jesus, 'can serve two masters . . . You cannot serve God and mammon' (Matthew 6.24). A man's god is that to which he gives himself, his time, his energy, his thought, his life, that which dominates and pervades his life. And if a man's one concern is with wealth, then wealth is his god.

(d) Whatever else is true, a man cannot take his wealth with him when he dies. He came naked into the world, and naked he will leave it (Job 1.21; Ecclesiastes 5.15,16; 1 Timothy 6.7). He will therefore be well advised to seek for the true riches, and to lay up the real treasure, which will last beyond time and into eternity. He should do good, and be rich in good deeds, and thus lay a foundation for the future life which is life indeed (1 Timothy 6.17,18).

As the New Testament sees it, and as experience confirms it, trust placed in any material thing is misplaced trust, and even in this life the mistake will be discovered. To see nothing beyond the material world is the way to disappointment in time and in eternity.

There is still certain material in the New Testament at which we must look before we begin to make our own general pattern.

i. There is a New Testament parable which has at least something to tell about Jesus' attitude to wealth—the parable of the rich man and Lazarus (Luke 16.19-31). This is the story of two men. One was rich. He was dressed in the finest clothes and ate the finest food; there was nothing in the world that he did not possess. The other was Lazarus, a beggar with ulcerated sores on his body, so helpless that he could not even keep off the dogs. Daily he was placed at the gate of the rich man's house and he did at least get the crumbs that fell from the rich man's table. Then the scene changes; it is no longer this world but the world to come. And in that other world the rich man is in agony and in torture, and the poor man is in bliss and blessedness—and there is no altering of their positions.

What is this parable saying? There has just been a reference in the preceding passage to the Pharisees 'who are lovers of money' (Luke 16.14). So this parable has something to say about money. What it is condemning so unsparingly is *irresponsibility*, lack of awareness, lack of concern. There is no indication that the rich man was in any way cruel to Lazarus in an active way. He let him lie there; he let him have the crumbs that fell from his table. The trouble was that he never noticed him. To the rich man Lazarus was part of the landscape. If ever he did notice him, it never struck him that Lazarus had anything to do with him. He was simply unaware of his presence, or, if he was aware of it, he had no sense of responsibility for it.

This parable is a vivid illustration of the fact that a man may well be condemned, not for doing something, but for doing nothing. As someone has put it: 'It was not what the rich man did that got him into gaol; it was what he did not do that got him into hell.' Hugh Martin writing on this parable in *The Parables of the Gospels* says that Dale called this parable 'the indignation of infinite love at white heat', and that Alexander McLaren called it 'the sternest of Christ's parables'. The condemnation is for the man who has money and who is quite unaware of those who have not, for the man who has no sense of responsibility for those who are less fortunate than he is. There is many a man who will spend on a dinner in a plush restaurant, even on the drinks at such a dinner, a sum exceeding the weekly old age pension for a man and wife. In one year Great Britain spent forty-five times as much on defence as it did on free aid to dependent territories. In one year something like £40,000,000 was given in such aid and something like £930,000,000 was spent in betting and gambling.

The New Testament unsparingly condemns irresponsibility, whether that irresponsibility be personal or national. It insists that no person or nation has a right to live in luxury while others live in poverty. It could be argued that we are forced to help others through the very heavy taxation system which now exists. This is perfectly true. But a fiscal obligation cannot take the place of a personal awareness. The simple fact, platitudinous as it may sound, is that no man has the right to live like the rich man while Lazarus is at his gates.

ii. The second passage which is very relevant for our discussion is the record of the cleansing of the temple by Jesus (Matthew 21.12,13; Mark 11.15,16; Luke 19.45,46; John 2.13-17). Here is the only incident in the New Testament when we find Jesus moved to violence; it must therefore have been an incident of special significance.

Jesus drove out of the temple courts the changers of money and the sellers of sacrificial victims. At the Passover time the temple tax was paid. The temple tax was about half a shekel. It does not sound much, but it has to be remembered that the average day's pay in Palestine in the time of Jesus amounted to about four new pence; and this means that the temple tax represented about two days' pay—a quite considerable sum. Since it was the ambition of every Jew to keep one Passover in Jerusalem the city was crowded with Jews who had come from all over the world. Since they came from all over the world, they brought all kinds of currency—Roman, Greek, Egyptian, Tyrian, Phoenician. For all normal purposes all the coinages were equally acceptable. But the temple tax had to be paid either in shekels of the sanctuary or Galilaean half-

158

shekels. This was because these were the only two coins which did not have a king's head on them. To the Jew a coin with a king's head on it was a graven image, especially if the king was deified. So the temple authorities had set up stalls in the temple where the other currencies could be changed into the right currency in which to pay the tax. It was on the face of it a convenient arrangement, but, for every coin changed the changers made a charge equivalent to about one new penny, and if the transaction involved the giving of change, another new penny was charged. So a pilgrim might well be charged an extra two new pence to enable him to pay his tax in the right currency—and remember that two new pence was about half a day's wage for a working man. It was blatant exploitation of simple people.

As for the sellers of pigeons, they had, if anything, an even better ramp. A man might bring his own pigeons to the temple to sacrifice, birds which he had bought outside. But every animal for sacrifice had to be without blemish and so there were temple inspectors, and if the animal had been bought outside the temple, they would certainly find a flaw in it and direct the worshipper to the temple stalls where victims which had already been examined were for sale. Again it seems a convenient arrangement, but outside the temple a pair of pigeons could cost as little as one new penny, and inside the temple they could cost as much as seventy-five new pence. Again it was sheer conscienceless exploitation, and exploitation practised in the name of religion.

Jesus was moved to the use of force. He whipped the sellers, put their animals out of the temple and overturned the tables of the money-changers. And what moved him to this violence was the sight of deliberate and highly profitable exploitation. The making of money by the exploitation of people's credulity or trustfulness, or, worse, by the exploitation of their need, incurs the wrath of Jesus—and it still happens.

iii. There is another parable of Jesus which has much to say about wealth, the strangest of all Jesus' parables, the parable in which every character is a rogue, the parable usually called the parable of the unjust steward (Luke 16.1-13). This parable tells how a steward was discovered to be dishonest and therefore faced the prospect of dismissal. In the east a steward had unlimited control over his master's property. So with the prospect of dismissal facing him, and with the end of his comfortable life in sight, this steward went one by one to the people who owed his master debts. He was not yet dismissed, and he had authority to deal with these debts and debtors. In each case he came to an agreement with the debtor to falsify the account. In each case the debt was recorded as considerably less than it was. In this way the steward hoped to be able to gain entry into the household of all the debtors in time to come, partly because they would be grateful to him, and no doubt partly—for he was a clever scoundrel—because, since he had made them sharers in his defalcations, he had them in his power. And when the master found out about it, instead of being angry, he looked on it as a clever bit of roguery, and congratulated the steward on his shrewdness in providing thus for his future.

That is an extraordinary parable. It is so extraordinary that it is clear that by the time Luke recorded it, its original lesson was lost, because Luke attaches no fewer than four different lessons to it—and all of them are relevant to the question of the Christian and his money. Let us look at the lessons which Luke has attached to it.

(a) He begins with the comment of the master: 'The sons of this world are wiser in their own generation than the sons of light' (Luke 16.8). What Luke means by this is that Christians would be very much better Christians if they were as keen to be Christians as the rascal of a steward was to cling on to his comfort and his money. It is perfectly true that this would be a very different world, and the church would be a very different church, if so-called Christians put as much time and thought and energy into being Christian as they do into making money, or even into practising a hobby or playing a game. If the

Christian put as much effort into maintaining his standards as a Christian as the worldly man puts into maintaining his standards of worldly comfort, he would be a very much better Christian than he is. There are things in which the children of this world can be an example to the children of light.

(b) His second comment is: 'And I tell you, make friends for yourselves by means of unrighteous mammon, so that when it fails, they may receive you into the eternal habitations' (Luke 16.9). This is a very difficult saying, but William Lillie seizes on one unmistakable thing about it. He says: 'Whatever else this means, it teaches that money is to be used as a means, and not as an end in itself' (William Lillie, *Studies in New Testament Ethics*, p. 97). It was not the money itself that the steward was interested in; he was interested in the friends which money could win him, and the comfort it could ensure for him. It is a cynical enough view of life—you can buy friendship, is the principle behind it—but the whole parable is designed to show how a cynical worldling can in some ways be an example to a Christian. So this tells us that money is meant to be used and not to be kept, and that it must never be regarded as an end in itself, but always as a means to an end—and the end towards which it is a means will be all important.

(c) The third lesson is: 'He who is faithful in a very little is faithful also in much; and he who is dishonest in a very little is dishonest also in much. If then you have not been faithful in the unrighteous mammon, who will entrust to you the true riches? And if you have not been faithful in that which is another's, who will give you that which is your own?' (Luke 16.10-12). This is a much simpler lesson. It is the principle that a man's conduct in money matters is no bad test of the man. If, we might almost say, a man can be trusted with money, he can be trusted with anything. A man's character, his honesty or his dishonesty, his straightness or his crookedness, can be seen, and nowhere better, in his daily business and financial dealings. The life a man lives in business is in its own way a preparation for eternal life.

(d) The fourth lesson is: 'No servant can serve two masters; for either he will hate the one and love the other, or he will be devoted to one and despise the other. You cannot serve God and mammon' (Luke 16.13). In Matthew this is part of the Sermon on the Mount, and appears in a quite different context (Matthew 6.24). We may well conclude that Jesus said this more than once. It says quite definitely that there is only room in life for one supreme loyalty, and that supreme loyalty must be to God. And, if a man's supreme loyalty is to God, there will never be anything wrong with either the way he makes his money or the way in which he spends it.

iv. The fourth place in which we will find guidance about the Christian and his money is the story of the collection which Paul made from the Gentile churches for the church at Jerusalem. This whole subject is dealt with most illuminatingly in *Christianity and the Affluent Society* by R. H. Fuller (pp. 46-59). With Paul, Christianity went out to the Gentiles. The day came when it became a kind of agreed division of labour that Paul should go to the Gentiles and that Peter and James and John should have the Jews as their special sphere. The one thing that the older apostles did enjoin upon Paul was to remember the poor, and that was something to which he required no urging (Galatians, 2.9,10). Some four or five years passed and Paul formed a scheme. Jerusalem was always a poor church, and Paul initiated a movement whereby all the Gentile churches he could contact would join in making a special gift collection for the church at Jerusalem. After all, Jerusalem was the mother church. It was from Jerusalem that the whole Christian religion flowed, and it was very right and proper that the younger churches, who had received such spiritual blessings from Jerusalem, should give Jerusalem all the material help they could. (The story can be pieced together from 1 Corinthians 16.1-4; 2 Corinthians 8 and 9; Romans 15.25,26.)

The first passage, short as it is, is very instructive for Christian giving through the church:

> On the first day of every week, each of you is to put something aside and store it up, as he may prosper, so that the contributions need not be made when I come (*1 Corinthians 16.2*).

Giving is to be *systematic* giving, so that there will not have to be a sudden emergency sermon and appeal. Far better a regular putting aside than a desperate effort when the deadline is fast approaching. The giving is to be *proportionate*. A man is to give as he prospers. The 'flat-rate' kind of giving is quite inappropriate, for what may be much for one man is likely to be negligible for another. The giving is to be *universal*. Each of them is to do it. So often the financial welfare of the congregation depends on the generosity of something under half of its members. It should be something in which all are involved, as they are able.

This collection for Jerusalem lay very near to Paul's heart. It was not only of great practical help to Jerusalem; it had a very great symbolic value for the whole church. It stood for at least three things.

(a) It symbolised the oneness of the church. It avoided any atmosphere of congregationalism. Just as there must be a relationship between individual and individual, so there must be a relationship between community and community, between congregation and congregation, between church and church. No congregation must think only of itself; it must be one for all and all for one. It is, for instance, very doubtful if wealthy congregations have any right to embark on schemes for things which are non-essentials, however much artistic value they may have, when there are congregations whose essential work is hindered through lack of funds. Any community whose outlook is limited to its own congregation is not a church.

(b) It symbolised the fact that no spectacular manifestation of spiritual gifts can take the place of concern for others. To put it technically, no number of *charismata*, spiritual gifts, can ever be a substitute for *agapē*, Christian love. The Corinthian church was taken up with spectacular things like speaking with tongues; and such things may well lead to spiritual pride, instead of love's concern.

(c) The third point is well made by R. H. Fuller. This collection symbolised the fact that spiritual fellowship, if it is really genuine, 'will always be given material expression, in terms of dollars and cents, of pounds, shillings and pence'. If we talk of the necessity of fellowship with others, that fellowship is quite unreal unless it issues in practical giving. James thought it the very negation of Christianity, if kind words and kind thoughts did not become concrete in kind deeds (James 2.14-17).

We have now looked at the biblical material about money and wealth and possessions. Let us go on to see if we can deduce from it certain general principles by which we may guide our own use of them.

i. We must right at the beginning dispose of the saying so common with preachers and evangelists that money does not matter, and that it is of no importance. It is very unlikely that anyone who has ever had the experience of having no money would ever say such a thing. Here is a letter which appeared some time ago in the correspondence columns of a newspaper:

Ask the man in the street, who has only a few shillings in his pocket, and who has to count every penny before spending it, if he is happy, and the answer will be, No. He'd be much happier being able to order a slap-up lunch and to buy a good suit, and only the possession of money can enable him to do so.

In all my life I have never met a needy person who was happy.

Lack of money is at the root of most marital problems too. It may be that that letter is too sweeping; but it has never been a pleasant thing to have too little, not to be able to get for one's family what other families get, not to be able to afford the occasional celebration or holiday, always to be haunted by a feeling of insecurity for the future. Even in the affluent society there are still people for whom life is like that. No honest person is going to say that money does not matter.

ii. If we assume that money and possessions must have a certain importance in life, we may go on to say that there is one basic principle which must govern our relationship to them. It is a test which goes as far back as the Greek philosophers. It is the question: *Do I possess my possessions, or am I possessed by them?* 'You cannot serve God and mammon,' the saying of Jesus has it (Matthew 6.24). The Greek word for *serve* is a strong word; it is *douleuein*, which comes from the word *doulos*, which means a *slave*. A man ought to be a slave to God, in the sense that in regard to God he should have no will of his own; he should regard himself as the possession of God; but a man should never be the slave of his possessions. And that is what some people are. Take away their luxuries and their comforts, and you take away their life. Their life is spent planning how they can maintain and increase their standards of comfort.

This is where the story of the rich young ruler comes in (Matthew 19.16-31; Mark 10.17-31; Luke 18.18-30). That story culminates in Jesus telling the young man that, if he wants the satisfaction he wistfully longs for, he must sell all that he has and give the proceeds to the poor, whereat he goes sorrowfully away for he was very wealthy. The question immediately arises: Is Jesus' command meant for everyone who wishes to be a Christian? Must every Christian give away all his possessions to the poor?

There is a very old Gospel called the Gospel according to the Hebrews. That Gospel may well be as old as some of our own Gospels. It never got into the New Testament; it is largely lost and only fragments remain. One of these fragments is in Origen's commentary on Matthew, and it is another version of this story. In it two rich men come to Jesus. The story runs:

The second of the rich men said to Jesus: 'Master, what good thing must I do to have life?' 'Fulfil the commandments of the Law and the Prophets,' Jesus said to him. 'I have done so,' the rich man answered. Jesus said to him: 'Go and sell everything you have, and distribute the proceeds to the poor, and come, follow me.' The rich man began to scratch his head, for he did not like this advice at all. The Lord said to him: 'How can you say, "I have kept the Law and the Prophets"? It is written in the Law that you must love your neighbour as yourself. And in point of fact many of your brothers, sons of Abraham, are clothed in filth and are dying of hunger, and your house is packed with good things, and not a single thing goes out of it to them.'

What was wrong with the rich young man was not his possessions, but his possessiveness. He was in fact possessed by his possessions. And the only cure for him was a radical change in his approach to the whole matter of possessions, a surgical eradication of the passion of possessiveness from his life. He claimed to have kept the commandments, and his claim was a lie, and his wealth was the very thing which prevented him from keeping them. If he had used his possessions to help and comfort others, this commandment would never have been given to him, but such was his possessiveness that he had either to abandon his possessions or abandon any attempt to follow the way of Jesus.

It is not wealth that is condemned; it is a certain attitude to wealth. It is the attitude in which a man has become so possessed by his possessions, so dominated by the desire to make and to have, to hold more and more, that a Christian use of possessions has become impossible for him.

iii. In the passage which follows the story of the rich young ruler it is not said that it is impossible for a rich man to get into the kingdom of God, but it is said that it is very difficult (Matthew 19.23-26; Mark 10.23-27; Luke 18.24-27). It is quite clear that money, wealth can be a real danger to a man's life.

It is a plain fact that the more money a man has, the more temptations he has. There are a great many things which are no temptation to a poor man because they are impossible for him. He has no temptation to luxurious living. Caviare and champagne are no temptation to a man who has all he can do to get bread and butter. It is no temptation to a man to keep two homes when it takes him all his time to keep one. There is no temptation to idleness to a man who simply cannot afford to take a day off work. It is the simple fact that there are many more sins available to the man who has money in his pocket. The possession of money can be a real test of a man's moral fibre. To say that we 'never had it so good' is also to say that we never had it so dangerous. The affluent society is also the society in peril. A new range of temptations opens to the man who can pay for them. The temptation to get drunk is only open to the man who can pay for enough liquor to get drunk. The more complex and sophisticated life becomes, the stronger its foundations must be. The wealthier a man is, the more he needs God. It is not the struggle with hard times that has brought disintegration to nations; it is the inability to cope with prosperity and luxury. Roman history tells the story of Hannibal, the great Carthaginian general, and his armies. He and his armies were well-nigh invincible. Then they spent one winter in Capua, that city where luxury and pride were notorious; and the army of Carthage was never the same again. The supreme danger comes when a man or a nation possesses things which it is not morally fit to possess. 'You've never had it so good' could end by being, not the proud claim of a politician, but the death sentence of a nation.

iv. Let us look more in detail at the dangers of wealth.

(a) It can beget a false sense of independence. A man can come to feel that he can buy his way into, or out of, anything. Sir Robert Walpole said that every man has his price, and there are those who consciously or unconsciously think that every situation has its price. It is quite true that there are doors which money can open and escape routes which money can supply; but a man will not come to the end of life without grimly discovering that there are some things which have no price-tag—and these things are the most important of all.

(b) There are times when money can cost too much. No traitor was ever happy. Judas Iscariot discovered this, when he discovered that the price of thirty pieces of silver was suicide (Matthew 27.3-5). There is a drug-market, a vice-market, a pornography-market, and money made on these markets costs too much. There is the wave of petty pilfering, which in industry alone is reckoned to cost £70,000,000 a year. There are expensive schools in which girls do not qualify for the school aristocracy until they have stolen something from a department store. George Macdonald told of a draper who made a fortune by keeping his thumbs inside the measure and so giving an inch or two short with every yard of cloth. 'He took from his soul,' said George Macdonald, 'and put it in his siller bag.' A fortune in money is a poor substitute for a man's soul.

(c) The more a man possesses in this world, the more difficult it will be for him to leave it. Jesus said: 'Where your treasure is, there will your heart be also' (Matthew 6.21). Once, after they had been to the house and policies of a wealthy man, Dr Johnson turned to his friend and said: 'These are the things which make it difficult to die.' A man can be so entangled with this world that he forgets that there is any other world.

(d) One of the curious results of wealth is that it is very liable to produce in a man, not the comfortable feeling that he has enough, but the constant desire for more. 'Enough', as someone said, 'is always a little more than a man has.' 'Riches', as the Roman proverb had it, 'are like salt water. The more you drink, the more you want to drink.' It is a curious thing that it may well happen that the more a man has, the more he will want to get, and the less he will want to give.

v. There remain five great principles to be stated, which, if they are kept in mind, will save any man from the dangers of wealth.

(a) *How did we get our money?* Did we get it in a way which harmed or injured no one, but helped and enriched the community? Did we get it in utter honesty, with every item open to the light of day? Did we get it without exploitation, and by giving value for it in honest work and service? Did we earn it always to the welfare and never to the hurt of the community, or of any individual in the community? To apply these tests would be never to go wrong in the getting of money.

(b) *How do we regard money?* Do we regard it as the *master* whom we serve? Do we regard it as an ascetic might do as an *enemy* with which we will have nothing to do? Or do we regard it as a *friend*, by the use of which we can enrich life for ourselves and for others?

Once Mr Okamura, the secretary of the Kobe YMCA, was telling that great Christian Kagawa about the difficulties of his association, about the debts which had accumulated, about the schemes which were frustrated for lack of money. Kagawa put his hand in his pocket, and took out a letter. The letter contained a cheque for £1,000 which Kagawa that morning had received from his publisher in payment for a book of his that was just about to be published. He handed the cheque to Okamura. Okamura said: 'I can't possibly take it.' Kagawa said: 'You must.' Kagawa literally forced it on him. Okamura went home and wrote a letter trying to get Kagawa to take the cheque back. 'You mustn't give money away like that,' he wrote. Kagawa wrote back: 'Why shouldn't I? When your friend is dying, there is only one thing to do— give him your life-blood.' If we regard money as something to be shared, it becomes our servant for good. If we regard it as something to be hoarded, it becomes our master. If we regard it as something to be used in love, it becomes one of the world's great powers.

(c) *How do we use money?* This has brought us inevitably to the question of how we use money. Do we use it selfishly? Do we make it to spend it on ourselves and on our family? Do we desire it to make life ever more lush for ourselves? When John Wesley was at Oxford his income was £30 a year. He lived on £28 and gave £2 away. His income later increased to £60, £90, £120 a year. He continued to live on £28 and to give the rest away. His rule was 'to *save* all I can that I may *give* all I can'. If a man's main question was, How much can I give? he would never go wrong.

(d) There is one principle which must never be lost sight of. People are always more important than things; men are always more important than money; workers are always more important than machines. This is exactly the principle that was lost sight of in the days of the industrial revolution. At that time working conditions, living conditions, wages conditions all took second place to production and profits. There were people who saw what was happening. It was argued that the cotton mills could not go on without child labour. Thomas Carlyle thundered: 'If the devil gets into your cotton mills, then close them.' It is for this disregard for people, for men and women, for basic human rights that we are suffering today in industrial suspicion and unrest. We can never even begin to have a proper view of money and possessions until we accept as a first principle the priority of persons. And this is not only good Christianity, it is also good economics, for in the end it is only the happy worker who is the good worker.

(e) There remains one last principle. There are times when to give money is not enough. To give money may be at times an evasion of a still greater responsibility. I am not one of these people who play down the generosity in giving of people with money by saying: 'It's easy to write a cheque.' It may be —but there are many who can write cheques, and who do not.

Nevertheless it must be said that there is need for something beyond impersonal giving. It was said of a man who was generous with money but who stopped there: 'With all his giving, he never gave himself.' And there are times when the giving of oneself is the greatest gift of all—for that is the gift that Jesus gave to men.

CHAPTER EIGHT

The Christian and the Community

Every man necessarily lives in two worlds. He lives within the four walls of the place that he calls home, and where his companions are the members of his own family. This is his private world. But equally a man has to go out of his house and home and has to live in a public world. He is not only a member of a family; he is also a member of a community, a state, a world. He is not only a private person; he is a public citizen.

A man's attitude to the world can take more than one form.

i. He can be totally immersed in the world. He can plunge into it and live as if there was no other world. His attitude may be: 'Eat, drink and enjoy yourself, for tomorrow we die.' 'Gather ye rosebuds while ye may,' as Herrick had it. Pile up kisses, as Catullus said, for when this world is done there remains nothing but a night which knows no ending and a sleep which knows no awakening.

But there is another way of being immersed in the world, and a commoner way than that. To be immersed in the world need not mean to be devoted to the pleasures of this world; it need not mean to eat and drink and be merry. There are many people who are immersed in this world in the sense that they are unaware that there is any other. They are not in the least immoral; they are not in the least dedicated to pleasure. They simply go in and out, and live decent respectable lives, and never think of any other world or any other life. They are hardly aware that there is any such thing as religion, or any such place as the church. They are not in the least hostile to religion. They regard it—if they think of it at all—as something which is quite irrelevant, something of which they have no need at all. A. J. Gossip used to say: You've seen a little evangelical meeting going on down some cul-de-sac of a street, while the crowds stream past on the pavements of the main road with never a look and never a second glance and never a thought. That is what the church is to many people—perhaps now to the majority of people. To be immersed in the world is not by any means necessarily to be a pleasure-lover; it is simply to be unaware of any horizons beyond this life.

ii. A man can take the opposite course and completely renounce this world. There has always been a strain of so-called Christian thought which had no use for this world at all; and there always have been people who quite deliberately and as completely as possible divorced themselves from the world. Thomas à Kempis said that the greatest saints deliberately avoided the society of men and tried to live to God and with God alone. The third and the fourth centuries were the great days of the monks and the hermits, when they deliberately turned their backs on life and on men and went to live in the desert, if possible not even within sight of another hermit.

There was one hermit who for fifty years lived on the top of Mount Sinai. He would not even see travellers and pilgrims who had come specially to visit him. 'The man who is often visited by mortals', he said, 'cannot be visited by angels.' There was the famous St Simeon Stylites, known as the pillarman. He tried living in a cavern; he tried digging a grave and living in it with nothing but his head exposed. Finally, in AD 423, he built himself a pillar six feet high and began to live on the top of it. He never came down. For no less than thirty-seven years he lived on the top of his pillar, which was gradually heightened until it was sixty feet high. He was the first of many pillar-saints who chose this way of isolating themselves from the world. There were the people called the shut-ins, the *inclusi*. They chose a niche in some monastery and literally got themselves bricked in, leaving only a narrow slit for the bare minimum of food and drink to be passed in to them. It is on record that one of them lived thus for twenty-five years. 'Are you alive?' someone asked through the narrow opening. 'I believe', he answered, 'that I am dead to the world.'

Men like these attempted to live as if the world did not exist. It was in many ways the most selfish of lives, for they were so concerned to save their own souls that they simply isolated themselves from all other men. They were, as it has been put, so heavenly-minded that they were no earthly use. Their renunciation was complete—and it was a caricature and parody of Christianity.

iii. So then there are people who are immersed in the world, and there are people who in the name of Christianity have renounced the world and who have as far as possible severed all connection with the world. From the point of view of the Christian ethic neither immersion in the world nor isolation from the world can be right. Jesus was quite clear that his men were not of this world (John 17.14,16). So much so were they not of this world that he warned them that the world would hate them as it had hated him (John 15.18,19; 17.14). It is therefore clear that no follower of Jesus can be immersed in the world. On the other hand, Jesus was equally clear that God loved the world (John 3.16). He did not pray that his men should be taken out of the world but that they should be kept from the evil of the world (John 17.15). And in the end he deliberately and of set purpose sent them out into the world (John 17.18).

The Christian must have an attitude to the world which combines involvement and detachment. This is not so unusual as it sounds. I think it would be true to say that this combination of involvement and detachment is characteristic of the work of many people, for instance, of the minister and of the doctor. Of course minister and doctor must be deeply involved, deeply identified with the people whom they wish to help. But they must at the same time be able to stand back and to view the facts in such a way that their judgment is not clouded by too much sentiment and too much softness. Sometimes it is necessary to be stern in order to be merciful and to be hard in order to be kind.

This involvement and detachment are characteristic of the Christian's attitude to the world. He is involved in the world and its life as Jesus was; but at the same time to him the world is not everything. It is the threshold to a larger and a wider life which begins when this life ends. In the world he lives, and lives to the full, but always with the conviction that it is something beyond this world which in the end gives this world its value and its significance.

Now we turn directly to the New Testament, and we are at once faced with the fact that the New Testament expects, and indeed demands, that a man should be a good citizen. Jesus was ready and willing to pay the temple tax that any Jew had to pay (Matthew 17.24-27). He does not question the fact that a man has a duty to the Emperor as well as having a duty to God, and that both must be fulfilled (Matthew 22.15-22).

Paul was proud to be a Roman citizen, and had no hesitation in claiming his rights as a citizen (Acts 21.39; 22.25). He writes to the Romans about the relationship of the Christian to the state, and he is quite clear that the state is a divine institution and that it is a Christian duty to give obedience to it. The magistrate is God's servant, and if a man does the right thing he has nothing to fear; it is only the criminal and the wrongdoer who have anything of which to be afraid. The taxes of the state ought to be paid and the authority of the state ought to be respected as Paul sees it (Romans 13.1-7). It is the duty of the Christian to remember in his prayers those who are in charge of public affairs from the Emperor downwards (1 Timothy 2.2). Peter is equally sure of the duty of citizenship. 'Fear God,' he says, 'and honour the Emperor' (1 Peter 2.17).

Then all of a sudden in the Book of the Revelation we get a thunderous volte-face, for in that book Rome is the great harlot, drunk with the blood of the saints and the martyrs (Revelation 17.1-7). The Roman Empire for the John of the Revelation has become the very essence and incarnation of devilish and Satanic power. What has happened? Why the difference?

In her great days, Roman justice and Roman impartiality were famous. The people whom Rome conquered were not resentful; they were grateful. The seas were cleared of pirates and the roads of brigands. A man might make his journeys in safety and live his life in peace, thanks to the *pax Romana*, the Roman peace. Quite spontaneously, men began to talk of Roma, the spirit of Rome, as something divine, and even as far back as the second century BC men were building temples for the worship of divine Rome. If things had stopped there, there might have been no great trouble. But it was the next step that made the difference. It is all very well to worship the spirit of Rome, but after all the spirit of Rome is an abstraction; and that abstraction is incarnated in the Emperor, and bit by bit the worship came to be transferred to the Emperor as the embodiment of Rome, and by the early days of the Christian era temples for the worship of Caesar the Emperor were quite common.

At first the Emperors really and truly did not want this. They were embarrassed with the whole business. But bit by bit the Roman state began to see a far-reaching use for this Caesar worship. The Roman Empire was a huge area stretching from the Danube to North Africa and from Britain to the Euphrates. It was very difficult to get some focus, some one thing, which would unify all the many tribes and nations in it. And suddenly the Roman government realised that they had just that in Caesar worship. We talk about the Crown being the one thing that holds the Commonwealth together; and it is just the same as if to unify the Commonwealth we set up a

176

universal worship of the Queen. So the Roman government laid it down in the end that every citizen should once a year burn a pinch of incense to Caesar and say: Caesar is Lord; and then he would get a certificate to say that he had done so. Be fair to Rome. After a man had done this he could go off and worship any god or goddess he liked, so long as the worship did not affect public order or public decency. The worship of Caesar was a test of a man's political loyalty far more than of his religion. But the one thing that the Christians would not say was: Caesar is Lord. For them, Jesus Christ is Lord— and no one else. So persecution broke out and as William Watson the poet put it:

> *So to the wild wolf hate were hurl'd*
> *The panting, huddled flock whose crime was Christ.*

And this is where the Revelation comes in. In Paul's time there was nothing like this. By the time of the Revelation compulsory Caesar worship was on the way.

All this has to be said, for the point is that the Christian is the good citizen, and the Christian is the obedient citizen— but there are limits and beyond these limits he will not go. In the Christian life there is only one supreme loyalty; that loyalty is to Jesus Christ, and that loyalty takes precedence over loyalty to family, loyalty to state, and loyalty to everything else, and so there can come a time when the Christian duty is disobedience to the state, and the Christian must hold that when that time comes he must act on it. It may not come once in a lifetime; it may not come once in a century— but it can come—and that is something which we cannot forget.

Let us then look at the relationship between the church and the Christian, and the state. That relationship has in its time taken many forms.

i. Sometimes the church has dominated the state. One of the great figures of the early church was Ambrose the Bishop of Milan. He was a close friend of Theodosius the Roman Emperor who was a Christian. Theodosius was a good and a generous man but he was cursed with a temper which at times made him act like a madman. There had been trouble in the city of Thessalonica, which resulted in the assassination of the governor. Theodosius reacted with violence. He waited until the people were gathered in the amphitheatre at the games; then he sent in his troops and 7,000 men, women and children were murdered where they stood. It was not long before the fiery tempered emperor repented of what he had done. He had in fact tried to cancel his order, but it was too late to do so. He came to Milan; he came to worship at the cathedral, for worship meant much to Theodosius; but Ambrose was standing at the cathedral door to bar his way. The bishop would not allow the emperor into the cathedral. For a year Theodosius had to do penance; for a year he was refused entry to the sacrament; and at the end of it he had to sit among the common penitents, and had even to lie prostrate in the dust before the cathedral door, before the bishop would accept him at all. There was a time when the Christian church could order the emperor of the world to lie prostrate in the dust.

The same happened to Henry the Second after the murder of Thomas Becket, the Archbishop of Canterbury. Becket had stood for the rights of the church. 'Who,' said Henry, 'will rid me of this turbulent priest?' Some of his courtiers took him at his word and murdered Becket in his own cathedral. The day came when Henry, clad in a hair-shirt, and living on bread and water, had to walk barefoot in the rain to the place where Becket had been murdered, and had to lie on the ground and be scourged by the bishop, the abbot and the priests, before he was received back into the church.

There have been times in history when the church dominated the state, and when kings and emperors bowed before an authority higher than their own. But these times are surely gone for ever, although we might argue that it was the church which even in our own day compelled the abdication of Edward the Eighth, because he wished to make queen a woman whom the church did not regard as a fit person to be queen of Britain. The church still has power, but not the utterly dominating power that once it had.

ii. There have been times when the church was utterly independent of the state, and when the church claimed that it was acting under an authority to which the state also was subject. This has been particularly the Scottish point of view. We see it fully displayed in John Knox's conflicts with Queen Mary. Mary resented his interference, but Knox's answer is: 'Outside the preaching place, Madam, I think few have occasion to be offended at me; and there, Madam, I am not master of myself, but must obey him who commands me to speak plain, and to flatter no flesh upon the face of the earth.' He is the bearer of a message from God and nothing and no one will stop him from delivering it. 'Yea, madam,' he says, 'it appertains to me to forewarn of such things as may hurt that commonwealth.' King and queen and commoner must listen to the conscience of the nation. The queen wept, but Knox makes answer: 'I must sustain your Majesty's tears, albeit unwillingly, rather than dare hurt my conscience, or betray my commonwealth through my silence.' The truth must be spoken. The Master of Maxwell warns him that, if he continues to oppose the queen, he will suffer for it. 'I understand not, Master, what you mean,' said Knox. 'I never made myself an adversary to the Queen's Majesty, except in the head of religion, and therein I think you will not desire me to bow.' When it comes to a message from God, come what may, that message must be given. One of the queen's councillors reminds him that he is not in the pulpit now but in the queen's presence. Knox thunders back: 'I am in the place where I am demanded of to speak the truth; and therefore I speak. The truth I speak, impugn it whoso list.' When the queen complains of the tone of his preaching, Knox tells her that as a man he may be no more than a worm, but he is a subject of this commonwealth, and God has given him an office which makes him 'a watchman over the realm and over the Kirk of God gathered in the same.' Here is the attitude that queen and commoner must listen to the word of God which must be spoken, and spoken without fear.

The classic expression of this is in the words of Andrew Melville to James the Sixth. The Commission of Assembly had appointed a deputation to visit the king at Falkland. There were James Melville, Patrick Galloway, James Nicolson and Andrew Melville. At first it was decided that James Melville should do the speaking, since he was likely to speak with a moderation to which the king might listen. But the king was 'crabbed and choleric' and Andrew Melville broke in. He caught the king by the sleeve, calling him 'God's silly vassal'. Then he said:

Sir, we will humbly reverence your Majesty always, namely in public, but since we have this occasion to be with your Majesty in private, and the truth is that you are brought into extreme danger of your life and crown, and with you the country and the Kirk of Christ is like to be wrecked, for not telling you the truth, and giving you a faithful counsel, we must discharge our duty therein, or else be traitors both to Christ and you! And, therefore, sir, as divers time before, so now again, I must tell you, there is two kings and two kingdoms in Scotland. There is Christ Jesus the King, and his kingdom the kirk, whose subject King James the Sixth is, and of whose kingdom not a king nor a lord nor a head, but a member.

It was in the same tone that Melville had already spoken to the Regent, the Earl of Morton. Morton had complained that Scotland would have no peace while Melville was there and had threatened him with exile. Melville replied:

Tush, sir! Threaten your courtiers in that fashion. It is the same to me whether I rot in the air or in the ground. The earth is the Lord's; my fatherland is wherever well-doing is

. . . Yet God be glorified, it will not lie in your power to hang nor exile his truth.

Here in the Scottish tradition is the complete independence of the church. It is not rebellion or revolution; it comes from the highest kind of loyalty, but it comes from the conviction that the differences are gone when men stand in the presence of God, and that God's man must speak no matter who is listening. King, queen and commoner are all subjects of God.

iii. There have been times when the church surrendered to the state and became subservient to the state. There is extant one extraordinary letter from Thomas Coke, John Wesley's right-hand man, written to the then Home Secretary Henry Dundas. The date is 8th November 1798. There was trouble in the Channel Islands. France was threatening invasion, and the able-bodied male population had been ordered to engage on military exercises on Sundays. Certain of the Methodists refused to exercise on Sundays; they were quite willing to do double time throughout the week but not—in their opinion—to desecrate the Sunday. Thomas Coke had many friends in high places, and he is writing to try to avert a bill which would institute real persecution against those who refused to exercise. He has no use at all for Democrats. 'When a considerable number of Democrats had crept in among us, to the number of about 5,000, I was a principal means of their being entirely excluded from our Society.' He has still less use for pacifists. 'The preamble of the Law, I think, says that some have refused to bear arms at all. I have heard of only one in Jersey who answered this description; and he has been already banished from the Island. We plead not for such. We look upon them at best to be poor Fanatics or arrant Cowards, and have no objection to their Banishment. They have no right to the protection of the Laws, who will not themselves be ready to protect those laws when in danger.' And then Coke astonishingly finishes: 'I can truly say, Sir, that though I very much love our Society, I love my King and Country

181

better' (John Vickers, *Thomas Coke, Apostle of Methodism*, p. 224).

A subservient church is a national disaster. It was said of Ambrose that he was 'the personified conscience of all that was best in the Roman Empire'. 'Who', he said to Theodosius, 'will dare to tell you the truth, if a priest does not dare?' The nation which has no independent church has lost its conscience.

iv. There have been times when the state refused the church any say at all in the affairs of the state, because the state held that such things were none of the church's business. When Hitler came to power, at first he did not threaten the church as such, but he took good care that no real Christian ever held any power. He deliberately got rid of them, for he openly admitted that he wanted no one in his government who knew any other loyalty than loyalty to the state.

When Niemöller, the great independent Christian, went to Hitler and told Hitler that he was troubled about the future of Germany, Hitler replied bleakly: 'Let that be my concern.' Goebbels, the notorious minister of propaganda, said to the church at large: 'Churchmen dabbling in politics should take note that their only task is to prepare for the world hereafter.' He had no objections to preachers being concerned with heaven so long as they left Germany alone.

Article 88 of the Constitution of the People's Republic of China states: 'Citizens . . . of China enjoy freedom of religious belief.' That means exactly what it says. There is no freedom to meet, to worship, to preach, to attempt to initiate any activity or to criticise any policy. So long as belief remains a purely internal thing which has no effect on conduct or relationships with other people or relationships with the state, there is freedom of *belief*. But if belief threatens to become action, then it is quickly strangled (Richard C. Bush Jr, *Religion in Communist China*, pp. 15-22).

In Victorian days Lord Melbourne made his famous state-

ment that religion is an excellent thing, so long as it does not
interfere with a man's private life. And the totalitarian states
have no objection to religion so long as religion keeps its
mouth shut about earth and confines itself to dreams of
heaven—and that, of course, reduces the church to a status
of sheer irrelevancy.

v. Lastly, we must look at the relationship of church and
state in the thought of Martin Luther, for it could well be said
that no view has had more influence on history, even in our
time, and no view has been more mistaken. We may find
Luther's view in two places. In the one place he divides
people into two groups; in the other he divides life into two
areas.

We may begin with his treatise on *Secular Authority; to
what extent it should be obeyed*, which was addressed to John,
Duke of Saxony, in 1523 (Volume 3 in the Philadelphia Edition
of the Works of Luther, pp. 228 *et seq.*; given most conven-
iently in E. G. Rupp and Benjamin Drewery, *Martin Luther*,
pp. 107-112). This divides people into two groups. There are
those who are true believers, and who belong to the Kingdom
of God, and those who are not believers and who belong to
the kingdom of the world. If all men were true Christians,
no king, lord, sword or law would be necessary. They would
do everything the law demands and more. On the other hand
there are those who do not accept Jesus Christ and his way.
'The unrighteous do nothing that the law demands, therefore
they need the law to instruct, constrain and compel them to do
good.' So for those who are not Christ's, 'God has provided
. . . a different government outside the Christian estate and
God's kingdom, and has subjected them to the sword, so
that, even though they would do so, they cannot follow their
wickedness, and that, if they do, they may not do it without
fear nor in peace and prosperity.'

It is impossible to try to rule the world by the gospel and its
love. If anyone tried to do so, 'he would loose the bands and
chains of the wild and savage beasts, and let them tear and

mangle everyone.' Before you can apply the Christian way to everyone, everyone must be a Christian—and to make everyone Christian is something that you will never accomplish. To attempt to govern the world by the gospel would be to act like a shepherd who put into the one fold wolves, lions, eagles and sheep all together, and told them to help themselves. The result would be chaos. Christians as Christians need no law, but the non-Christian does. Therefore the sword is necessary. 'Because the sword is a very great benefit and necessary to the whole world, to preserve peace, to punish sin and to prevent evil, he (the Christian) submits most willingly to the rule of the sword, pays tax, honours those in authority, serves, helps, and does all he can to further the government, that it may be sustained and held in honour and fear.' The Christian is therefore under obligation to serve and to cherish the sword of government, just as he serves and cherishes any other of the divinely given institutions of life, such as matrimony or husbandry. 'There must be those who arrest, accuse, slay and destroy the wicked, and protect, acquit, defend and save the good.'

So then it is Luther's argument that so long as there are two kinds of people—those in and those not in the kingdom of God—it is impossible to arrange society on the principles of Christian love. There must be law and force; there must be the sword of the magistrate. And in order to see that there is safety and good order the Christian is bound to respect and honour and, if he is qualified, to serve the state. 'Therefore, should you see that there is a lack of hangmen, beadles, judges, lords or princes, and find that you are qualified, you should offer your services and seek the place, in order that necessary government may by no means be despised and become inefficient or perish.' Quite simply, Luther is saying that you cannot govern an unchristian world by Christian love, and in such a world you have to use the sword and all that the sword stands for against the wicked man.

The second passage is much more far-reaching. It is contained in Luther's sermons on the Sermon on the Mount (*Luther's Works*, the American Edition, vol. 21, pp. 106-115). This is from a sermon on Matthew 5.38-42, where Jesus teaches us to abandon the principle of an eye for an eye and a tooth for a tooth, and tells us not to resist evil, but to turn the other cheek, to give the cloak as well as the coat, and to go not one mile but two.

In this sermon Luther's point is that the Christian lives in two spheres. In this passage, Luther says, Jesus is teaching how the individual Christian must live *personally*. As a Christian individual, apart from his official position, Christians 'should not desire revenge at all. They should have the attitude that, if someone hits them on one cheek, they are ready, if need be, to turn the other cheek to him as well, restraining the vindictiveness not only of their fist but also of their heart, their thoughts, and all their powers as well.' The Sermon on the Mount is for the Christian as a person and as an individual.

But the Christian is not only an individual person; he is a *person in relationship*; and here the situation is very different. Luther's point of view is so important that we must allow him to speak for himself, and we must quote him at length:

There is no getting around it, a Christian has to be a secular person of some sort. As regards his own person, according to his life as a Christian, he is in subjection to no one but Christ, without any obligation to the emperor or to any other man. But at least outwardly, according to his body and property, he is related by subjection and obligation to the emperor, inasmuch as he occupies some office or station in life or has a house and a home, a wife and children; for all these are things which pertain to the emperor. Here he must necessarily do what he is told and what this outward life requires. If he has a house or a wife or children or servants, and refuses to support them, or, if need be, to

185

protect them, he does wrong. It will not do for him to declare that he is a Christian and therefore has to forsake
or relinquish everything. But he must be told: 'Now you
are under the emperor's control. Here your name is not
"Christian", but "father" or "lord" or "prince". According
to your own person, you are a Christian; but in relation
to your servant you are a different person and you are
obliged to protect him.'

You see, now we are talking about a Christian-in-relation;
not about his being a Christian, but about this life and his
obligation in it to some other person, whether under him
or over him or even alongside him, like a lord or a lady,
a wife or children or neighbours, whom he is obliged,
if possible, to defend, guard and protect. Here it would
be a mistake to teach: 'Turn the other cheek, and throw
your cloak away with your coat.' That would be ridiculous,
like the case of the crazy saint who let the lice nibble at
him and refused to kill any of them on account of this
text, maintaining that he had to suffer and could not resist
evil.

And then there comes the passage which is the crux of the
whole matter:

Do you want to know what your duty is as a prince or a
judge or a lord or a lady, with people under you? You do
not have to ask Christ about your duty. Ask the imperial
or the territorial law. It will soon tell you your duty toward
your inferiors as their protector. It gives you both the power
and the might to punish within the limits of your authority
and commission not as a Christian but as an imperial
subject.

Luther then quotes the case of those who were called to arms
by infidel emperors.

In all good conscience they slashed and killed, and in this
respect there was no difference between Christians and
heathen. Yet they did not sin against this text. For they

were not doing this as Christians, for their own persons, but as obedient members and subjects, under obligation to a secular person and authority.

So,

When a Christian goes to war or when he sits as a judge's bench, punishing his neighbour, or when he registers an official complaint, he is not doing this as a Christian, but as a soldier or a judge or a lawyer ... A Christian should not resist any evil; but within the limits of his office, a secular person should oppose every evil. The head of a household should not put up with insubordination or bickering among his servants. A Christian should not sue anyone, but should surrender both his coat and his cloak when they are taken away from him; but a secular person should go to court if he can to protect and defend himself against some violence or outrage. In short the rule in the Kingdom of Christ is the toleration of everything, forgiveness, and the recompense of evil with good. On the other hand, in the realm of the emperor, there should be no tolerance shown to any injustice, but rather a defence against wrong and a punishment of it, and an effort to defend and maintain the right, according to what each one's office and station may require.

It is quite true that Luther does in the treatise—but not in the sermon—indicate that there are limits, and that the prince has no right to demand that which is wrong. But this is not the main impression which his teaching leaves. His teaching leaves the impression that in the secular realm the government is supreme, and that from it, and not from Christ, the Christian must take his duty. And it is this very fact which allowed Hitler to come to power and begat Belsen and Dachau.

The Lutheran church did not stand out, for it was conditioned to accept the civil power.

The whole thing is to be seen at its most terrible in Luther's attitude to the Peasants' Revolt in 1524-5. The peasants revolted. They had therefore in Luther's eyes broken the command of Jesus to render to Caesar the things that are Caesar's (Matthew 22.21). They had broken the scriptural law regarding obedience to the state as Paul stated it in Romans 13. They have therefore, in Luther's words, 'forfeited body and soul, as faithless, perjured, lying, disobedient knaves and scoundrels are wont to do.' They are makers of sedition and therefore outside the law of God and the empire. In regard to any peasant, 'The first who can slay him is doing right and well . . . Therefore let everyone who can, smite, slay, and stab, secretly or openly, remembering that nothing can be more poisonous, hurtful, or devilish than a rebel. It is just as when one must kill a mad dog.' They can be slaughtered without even a trial. 'Here there is no time for sleeping; no place for patience or mercy. It is the time of the sword, not the day of grace . . . Strange times, those, when a prince can win heaven with bloodshed, better than other men with prayer!'

It might not be too much to say that Luther's ethic of church and state was the greatest disaster in all the history of ethics, for it opened the way for a kind of Christianity which allowed the state to do terrible things, and in too many cases made no protest. It is impossible to divide life into spheres like that. A Christian is a Christian in any sphere of life, and in things sacred and things secular alike Jesus Christ is Lord for him.

It would not be right to leave the matter thus vague and abstract and generalised. We have to ask ourselves just where the Christian ethic may in fact have to show itself. I think that there are three areas in modern life where there is special need for Christian ethical witness.

i. The first is the area of *racialism*. There are certain simple facts which will show how real this problem is. There are one million coloured immigrants in Britain already. By 1980 the number will naturally increase to three million. There are something like 15,000 university students and 48,300 students from overseas in the technical colleges. Two per cent of the post-graduate students in the country are from overseas. At the present time 3 per cent of the school-leavers are coloured; by the mid-seventies that number will rise to 15 per cent. And now here is the really serious fact. Youth employment officers state that they have to spend as much time placing immigrant school-leavers in jobs as they have to spend searching for suitable jobs for handicapped children. It is almost as difficult for a coloured person to find work as it is for a handicapped person (R. H. Fuller and B. K. Rice, *Christianity and the Affluent Society*, p. 137). Fuller and Rice record a curious kind of parallel problem. In India today there are two million unemployed high-school graduates and 200,000 unemployed BA's. The racial problem is not something that can wait.

There is a very real sense in which the ancient world was a divided world. It was particularly so in two areas. The Jew was divided from the Gentile. To a Jew a Gentile child was unclean from birth. 'The daughter of an Israelite may not assist a Gentile woman in childbirth since she would be assisting to bring to birth a child for idolatry.' Even in the commonest things of life this appeared. A Gentile might not cut the hair of a Jew. A Jew could not eat bread baked by a Gentile or drink milk from a cow milked by a Gentile, unless a Jew was present at the milking. Suspicion of the Gentiles was acute. 'Cattle may not be left in the inns of the Gentiles since they are suspected of bestiality; nor may a woman remain alone with them since they are suspected of lewdness; nor may a man remain alone with them since they are suspected of shedding blood.' (The quotations are from the Mishnah tractate *Abodah Zarah* 2.1,2,6.)

There was the division between the Greek and the barbarian. Originally to the Greek the barbarian was a man who spoke another language, a man who unintelligibly said *bar bar*, barking like a dog, instead of speaking the beautiful and flexible Greek language. We twice get that meaning in the

New Testament as the translation of the Authorised Version makes clear. In the First Letter to the Corinthians Paul is speaking about the gift of speaking with tongues and about its unintelligibility, and he says: 'Therefore if I know not the meaning of the voice, I shall be unto him that speaketh a barbarian, and he that speaketh shall be a barbarian unto me' (1 Corinthians 14.11 AV). In the narrative of the shipwreck in Acts Luke tells how Paul and his party were shipwrecked on Malta and then goes on to say: 'And the barbarous people showed us no little kindness' (Acts 28.2). A barbarian in Greek was often simply a man who spoke an unintelligible language. But the word came to indicate not simply a person who spoke a different language, but a person from an inferior culture. So Heraclitus can speak of people with 'barbarian souls'. The barbarian was different from the Greek. And so the great Greek writers like Plato, Demosthenes, Isocrates can use a series of phrases. They can say that the barbarians are 'foes by nature'; that they are 'natural and hereditary foes'; that they are foes 'by nature and tradition'; that between them and the Greek there is a 'perpetual and truceless warfare' (cf. T. J. Haarhoff, *The Stranger at the Gate*, pp. 8,13, 60,61,65,66). But there was another side to the Greek, and to the Roman. Terence, the Roman dramatist could say: 'I regard no human being as a stranger.' Diogenes could claim to be a citizen of the world. He may have invented the word *cosmopolitan*. Alexander the Great could talk of his desire to marry the East to the West, and to mingle as in one great loving-cup all the races of mankind.

In the ancient world there was division all right; there were cleavages; but there was no colour-bar as such. There were divisions of religion, of culture, of tradition; but the sheer contempt for a man as a human being, which is the basis of the colour-bar, was not there—and it is here today, and not only in South Africa.

The area of racial relationships is another area in which men have sown the wind and are reaping the whirlwind. Many years ago now an authoress called Janet Mitchell wrote a book which included an account of a visit to America. One of the high-lights of her tour was to be a visit to Paul Robeson, the great singer and actor, to whom she had an introduction. She was staying with friends in Chicago, and she was talking enthusiastically of her coming visit to Paul Robeson. She noticed that the atmosphere had become a little chilly. 'What's the matter?' she asked. Her friends answered: 'We wouldn't talk too much about visiting Paul Robeson, if we were you.' 'Why on earth shouldn't I talk about it?' Janet Mitchell said. 'He's one of the greatest singers and actors in the world.' 'That may be,' her host answered. 'But Paul Robeson's a nigger.' If you treat any man or any body of men like that, you are building up a store of trouble that is some day going to erupt—and it has erupted.

Somewhere I read the story of an artist who was commissioned to design a stained-glass window illustrating the children's hymn:

> *Around the throne of God in heaven*
> *Thousands of children stand,*
> *Singing, Glory, glory, glory.*

The design was finished; the painting which had to serve as a pattern for the window was completed, and the committee in charge were to see it next day. That night the artist had a dream. He saw in the dream a stranger in his studio, and the stranger was working with brushes and palette at his picture. 'Stop!' he shouted. 'Stop! You'll spoil my picture!' The stranger turned. 'It is you,' he said, 'who have spoiled it.' 'I?' said the artist. 'I spoil my own picture?' 'Indeed you have,' said the stranger. 'How do you make that out?' said the artist. And the stranger answered: 'Who told you that the faces of all the children in heaven were white? Look! I am putting in the little black faces, and the brown ones and the yellow ones.' Morning came. The artist woke and rushed into his studio. The picture was as he had left it. He seized his brushes and paints and sketched in the faces of the children of every colour and of every nation. And when the committee saw it later in the morning, they said: 'Perfect! It's just what we wanted! It's God's family at home!' Who indeed said that the faces of all the children in God's family are white?

All this is true, but I do not think that it would be fair to leave things there like that. You cannot settle this matter on a wave of emotion; there is more to it than that. I can say in principle that racialism is entirely wrong, and that integration is entirely necessary, but I do not know how I might feel if I lived in a country in which the white population was in a tiny minority. But this we can say with certainty. There should and there must be equality of opportunity and equality of treatment for all. This might well mean that immigration into any country might need to be controlled, until the country can absorb the newcomers; until they can be properly housed; until there are decent jobs for them to do; and until they can be truly integrated into its education and its work and its life. But, if the principle is accepted that man as such is dear to God, the right way to treat him will soon be worked out.

ii. The second area in which the Christian must demonstrate the Christian ethic is in the area of *social conditions*, in the social environment in which he lives.

It is here that the church has much to live down. There is no doubt that for long the church was connected with the establishment and with the *status quo*. The church was held to be, and appeared to be, the supporter of things as they are. It had in the nineteenth century much to do with the upper and the middle classes, and little to do with the working man.

One of the most terrible things I ever read is in William Purcell's life of Studdert Kennedy. In the days of Kennedy's father, in the time of the industrial revolution, in the square of St Peter's church in Leeds, a poor wretched man publicly burned the Bible and the Prayer Book, because he felt that the church was more than anything else responsible for the conditions in which he had to live. It was at that time that a country farm-labourer was asked if he attended the Communion, and answered: 'No. That kind of thing is for the gentry'—and the tragedy is that it was very largely true, before John Wesley came.

The social gospel is not an addendum to the gospel; it is the gospel. If we read the Gospels, it becomes clear that it was not what Jesus said about God that got him into trouble. What got him into trouble was his treatment of men and women, his way of being friendly with outcasts with whom no respectable Jew would have had anything to do. It has always been fairly safe to talk about God; it is when we start to talk about men that the trouble starts. And yet the fact remains that there is no conceivable way of proving that we love God other than by loving men. And there is no conceivable way of proving that we love men other than by doing something for those who most need help.

What then is the Christian duty now? The Christian duty depends on one principle which cannot be evaded. If we think that conditions should be changed, if we think that in any area of life conditions are not what they should be in a so-called Christian country, then there is only one way to alter them—through political action. There is no other possible way through which the change can be effected. And this leaves us facing the inevitable and inescapable conclusion—the Christian ought to be deeply involved in politics. He ought to be active in local government; he ought to be an active member of his trade union; he ought to be active and responsible in national politics. This is not to say that he is to be a member of any particular political party, for no party has a monopoly of what is right. The Christian should be in all parties, acting everywhere as the conscience of the community and the stimulus to action.

We often complain of the action of local government and of trade unions; it is a first principle that no man has a right to complain of the work of others, unless he is prepared to do it better himself. It is the simple fact that time and time again decisions are taken and issues are settled by a small and militant minority who are there, while the rest absent themselves and refuse to accept their responsibilities. We cannot complain, if we leave it to others to take the decision in which we should ourselves have shared. No leaven ever leavened any loaf unless it got inside it; and the Christian will never be the leaven of society until he is completely involved in it. Luther once said an extraordinary thing in his treatise *Concerning Christian Liberty*. He thinks of all that God has given him in Christ; and then he thinks of the obligation that this love and this generosity have laid upon the man who has accepted them, especially the obligation to be among men as one who serves, as Jesus was. Then he says: 'I will therefore give myself as a sort of Christ to my neighbour, as Christ has given himself to me; and will do nothing in this life except what I see will be needful, advantageous and wholesome for my neighbour, since by faith I should abound in all good things in Christ.' Here is the voice of the man who *must* give himself to the community. Every Christian ought to feel like that, and therefore every Christian ought to give himself to the service of the community in which he lives.

iii. The third area in which the Christian ethic is involved is the area of *war*.

In the ancient world war was a very gentlemanly engagement; it was fought by mercenaries, who had their rules and kept them. It is on record that during one campaign it was discovered that in a house between the armies there was a picture by Polygnotus, the greatest of the Greek artists. The war was suspended until the picture had been removed to a place of safety. But the very nature of war has changed. During the Spanish Civil War a journalist described a city street, bombed, littered with broken glass and all kinds of debris. Along the street came a little boy dragging a wheelless wooden engine at the end of a piece of string. There is a burst of fire and a scurry; and when the dust settles the boy is dead. That is war.

But not even that is war today. That bears no relationship to the potential of modern warfare. Something happened at Hiroshima and Nagasaki, something after which the world can never be the same again. A method of fighting was discovered and used which could kill thousands, which could lay waste a city, and which could cause genetic damage to generations yet unborn. It is said—and it is unquestionably true—that this country and America and the Western democracies at least would never use the atomic bomb as an offensive weapon, and have it only as a defensive deterrent. But one thing is clear—it is not a deterrent, *unless in certain circumstances the nation possessing it is prepared to use it*. And this is exactly what I believe a Christian can never consent to do. I can in no circumstances conceive it to be in accord with Christian principles to use such methods.

If I am asked if I would defend my wife or my daughter or anyone else if I saw them attacked, the answer of course is, Yes. And the difference is this. In such a case I would be dealing with the person who was committing the assault. And there is no possible relationship between dealing with a criminal in the act of his crime and raining death and destruction over thousands of people completely indiscriminately, and so killing men, women and children, without distinction.

We are told that we must not kill. That commandment is not abrogated when the killing is not individual but mass murder. We are told that we must defend Christianity—or Western civilisation—as if they were the same thing—from forces which might destroy it. In the first place, I do not believe that Christianity can be destroyed. In its early days it survived the whole might of the Roman Empire and emerged. In the second place, if Christianity has to be defended by such means, then I for one would want nothing to do with it. It is impossible to defend the faith whose watchword is love and whose emblem is a man upon a cross, by a policy of destruction. I do not love my enemies when I drop a bomb on them. And—in the end—it may seem a naïve statement, and it may seem an oversimplification, but I cannot imagine Jesus in any circumstances pressing the switch which would release a bomb. I think that the time has come for the Christian and the church to say that they are finished with war.

The Christian both as a man and as a Christian must be involved in the community. It was never more difficult to be a Christian within the community than today—and it was never more necessary.

CHAPTER NINE

Person to Person Ethics

There never was an age in history when it was so difficult for a person to remain pure and chaste and good as it is today.

That is the first sentence that I wrote to begin this talk tonight; but no sooner had I written it than I began to doubt very much if it is true. The proverb has it that the more things change, the more they remain the same; and the plain fact of history is that it has never been easy to be good and to be pure and to be chaste. So, then, I want to begin by looking at the world into which Christianity came, and to see what the person to person ethic was like in it. I want to take only certain typical incidents and sayings from that ancient world, and it is because they are typical—not because they are unusual—that I take them.

First of all, let us look at Greece. In one of his speeches (*Against Naeaera* 122) Demosthenes sets out what he takes to be the rule of life. Demosthenes did not say this because he was condemning it, or because it was unusual, but because he was stressing that it was normal day-to-day practice:

> We keep prostitutes for pleasure; we keep mistresses for the day-to-day needs of the body; we keep wives to be the mothers of our children and the guardians of our home.

In Greece relationships before marriage and outside marriage were the normal practice, an accepted part of life. It is the supreme ordinariness of the thing which makes it so shocking.

Second, let us turn to Rome. Let us take the case of Messalina in Rome as Juvenal the Roman satirist tells it to us—and remember it is not a Christian moralist but a Roman poet who

197

is telling the story. Messalina was no less a person than the Empress of Rome, the wife of Claudius the Emperor. She would, says Juvenal, wait until Claudius was asleep. Then with one maid and a night-cowl over her head she would slip out to her own special cell in the public brothels and serve there as a common prostitute. I quote: 'There she stood with nipples bare and gilded . . . Here she graciously received all-comers, asking from each his fee; and when at last the keeper dismissed his girls, she remained to the very last before closing her cell, and, with passion still raging hot within her, went sorrowfully away. Then, exhausted by men but unsatisfied, with soiled cheeks and begrimed with the smoke of the lamps, she took back to the imperial pillow all the odours of the stews' (Juvenal, *Satires* 6.114-132). A Roman Empress delighting to act as a common prostitute—and, just about AD 50—that is the world into which Christianity came.

Third, let us look at divorce in that ancient world. Broadly speaking, there was no process of divorce; all that a husband had to do was to tell his wife to go, for in that ancient world a woman was a thing, not a person, and had no legal rights at all. In the Roman world divorce was staggeringly common. Seneca said that women were married to be divorced and were divorced to be married (*De Beneficiis* 3.16). He said that women counted the years by the names of their husbands rather than by the names of the consuls. Hiberina, says Juvenal, naming a reigning beauty, would as soon be satisfied with one husband as with one eye (*Satires* 6.53,54). Martial tells of a woman who was living with her tenth husband (Martial, *Epigrams* 6.7). Juvenal tells of a woman who had eight husbands in five years (Juvenal, *Satires* 6.230). And Jerome tells us of what must have been the unsurpassable record, the case of a woman who was married to her twenty-third husband, she being his twenty-first wife (Jerome, *Letters* 2).

Fourth, we turn to the Jewish world. There is not in the

Jewish world the same all-embracing immorality; but the state of divorce was serious. Jesus forbade divorce, except for the case of adultery (Matthew 5.32; 19.9; Mark 10.11,12; Luke 16.18; I Corinthians 7.10,11). The Jewish law was clear. It is stated in Deuteronomy 24.1-4 that a man can give his wife a bill of divorce, if he has found some matter of uncleanness or some indecency in her. The bill of divorce was no more than a single sentence dismissing her and giving her freedom to marry anyone who would have her. Now, of course, everything depends on the interpretation of the phrase *some matter of uncleanness*. And on this in Judaism in the time of Jesus there were two schools of thought. There was the school of Shammai, which said exactly the same as Jesus, that adultery was the only possible ground of divorce. But there was the school of Hillel, and it said that *a matter of indecency* could mean going out with her hair unbound, spinning in the street, talking to another man, spoiling his dinner, speaking disrespectfully of her husband's parents in her husband's presence, being a scolding woman (and a scolding woman was defined as a woman whose voice could be heard in the next house!) (Ketuboth 7.6; Gittin 9.10). It is easy to see which school would be most popular, and in Palestine in the time of Jesus girls were afraid to marry because the tenure of marriage was so insecure.

It is, of course true that in every age and generation and in every society there have always been people living in honour and in fidelity and in purity and in chastity; but in the days of the first Christians the atmosphere was such that it can have been no easy task to escape the moral infection which pervaded society.

It is further to be added that the ancient world was riddled with homosexuality. It would be difficult to name one of the great Greeks who did not practise this kind of love—Plato, Aristotle, Sophocles and even the great Socrates. The thing had reached such a stage in Greece that when Plato talks of love it is homosexual love he means. The ordinary love of

women was regarded as low and dishonourable and for a
man of culture only the love of a boy was considered worthy.
It is a simple fact that of the first fifteen Roman Emperors
fourteen were practising homosexuals. It is not for nothing
that Paul warned his people against it (Romans 1.26,27; I
Corinthians 6.9; I Timothy 1.10). It would be hard for a man
in New Testament times to regard as wrong that which the
greatest and the wisest practised.

When we look back on those early days, we can see that
we are not really called upon to face anything that previous
generations have not faced. So then let us look at some of the
areas of this person to person ethic.

i. Let us begin by looking at the sphere of the family. Someone has said that what life does to us, everyone of us, is
equivalent to dropping us down the chimney of some house at
random, landing us in the middle of a group of people, and
then saying: 'Get on with these people as well as you can.'
The problem of the family is quite simply the problem of
living together.

When we study the New Testament family ethic, the first
thing that strikes us about it is that in every case it is what
can only be called a reciprocal ethic. This is to say that no
privilege is ever given without a corresponding responsibility.
In the New Testament family ethic the duty is never, literally
never, all on one side. So wives have to obey their husbands,
but the husband is always to treat the wife with love and with
consideration. Children are to obey their parents, but parents
are never to behave unreasonably to their children in such a
way as to anger or discourage them. Always there is a double
duty; never is the duty all on one side (Ephesians 5.21-6.9;
Colossians 3.18-4.1).

In the family there are two main relationships. First, there
is the relationship of parent and child. On the side of the
parent, there are two main things to be said. The first is quite
simply that those of us who are parents must always remember
that times do change. A certain famous authoress tells how

200

once she said to her small daughter: 'When I was your age, I was never allowed to do a thing like that.' And the child answered: 'But you must remember mother that you were *then* and I'm *now*.' There is a *then* and there is a *now*, and they are not the same, nor can they be made the same. The parent has to remember all the time that he cannot keep things as they are.

The second is even more important. When Paul was writing to the Colossians his plea to parents is to avoid treating their children in such a way that the children become discouraged (Colossians 3.21). It may well be that this is the most important rule of family life. The child may come to feel that the parent is always 'going on' at him—and often he is not far wrong. What most human beings, young or old, need in this world more than anything else is encouragement. Benjamin West became one of the great British painters, and he tells us how. When he was young his mother went out, leaving him in charge of his little sister Sally. In the absence of his mother the boy came across some bottles of coloured ink and some brushes and he was determined to try to paint a picture of his little sister Sally. The result may well be imagined; there was ink here, there, and everywhere. His mother came back to the house; she took one look at the mess and she took one look at the boy's attempted picture. 'Why,' she said, 'it's Sally!' And she took Benjamin in her arms and kissed him. And as Benjamin West said all his life afterwards: 'My mother's kiss made me a painter.' If she had done what so many of us would have been tempted to do, there might have been no Benjamin West. Our first instinct to those who are young should be encouragement. We do not realise how much the young person worries with the modern tensions in education and in life. In the 15-19 age-group suicide is the third most common cause of death. And one of the greatest encouragements is simply to treat the child as a reasonable human being. The days of doing a thing 'because I say so' are long past. Anyone will obey more quickly and act better, if he

201

does so intelligently, and if he knows and understands why the order is given.

In the sphere of parent and child, the young person should remember the duty of gratitude. It is the plain fact of nature that of all creatures man takes the longest before he can sustain his own life, and there are long years when, not positive injury, but simple neglect would have killed us. Only love can repay love, and yet it happens again and again within the family that we hurt most of all those whom most of all we ought to cherish. When James Barrie looked back across the years to his relationship with his mother Margaret Ogilvie, he said: 'When I look back, I cannot see the smallest thing undone.' I do not think that I ever met anyone who could say that—but that is the aim. For one of the saddest things in life is to look back and to say: 'If only I had done this or that . . .'

One last thing, in regard to the parent-child, child-parent relationship. A home should be a place from which the child is equipped to go out, and to which he will always return. Some parents find it very hard to grasp the fact that their basic duty is to enable the child to leave them and to live his own life. Smother-love and mother-love can be very easily confused. If we bring up our children in such a way that they are eager to go out and glad to return, then our task will be well done.

ii. The second area of the home and family life is marriage. There is no doubt that for the Christian ethic in its ideal form, marriage is given for life. In the Mark account of the words of Jesus (Mark 10.1-12) no exception at all is made to that rule. In the parallel Matthew account (Matthew 5.32) the one exception is divorce for infidelity.

We have to have a care what we do here. First, we have to face the fact that sexual infidelity is far from being the only thing that can wreck a marriage. It is one of the curious facts of language that the word *immorality* has come almost exclusively to mean sexual immorality. There is many a person in marriage who is blameless from the legal sex point of view, but who has nonetheless succeeded in making marriage a hell for the other partner. Fletcher quotes a passage from Dorothy Sayers:

A man may be greedy and selfish; spiteful, cruel, jealous and unjust; violent and brutal; grasping, unscrupulous, and a liar; stubborn and arrogant; stupid, morose, and dead to every noble instinct; and yet, if he practises his sinfulness within the marriage bond, he is not thought by some Christians to be immoral (J. Fletcher, *Moral Responsibility* pp. 133, 134).

There are other things than adultery which can kill a marriage and the love which should be in it.

The second thing we have to be careful about is that we do not try to make the words of Jesus into a law, and thus forget that the greatest thing of all is love. We have always to remember that we have to take to any situation the whole of the message of Jesus, not just one sentence from it. I am not thinking of the kind of situation in which two people have entered into marriage without thought and without facing the realities; nor am I thinking of the kind of situation in which the partners in a marriage wish to break the marriage up simply because the initial romance and glamour are gone, and they have not the moral fibre and the staying power to face the routine of the every day. I am not thinking of the kind of situation in which people think of life together in terms of soft lights and sweet music and never realise until too late that there are such things as kitchen sinks, and pots and pans, and crying babies and washing of nappies. Still less am I thinking of the kind of situation in which one of the partners of the marriage allows a relationship to develop which is in itself the way to disloyalty.

But if it should so happen that two people find living together an impossibility; if they have consulted the doctor and the minister or the priest and the psychologist and the psychiatrist; if they have taken all the guidance that there is to take, and if the situation is still beyond mending, then I do not think that it is an act of Christian love to keep two such people tied together in a life that is a torture; nor do I think that it is right for them only to be allowed to separate and never to be allowed to try to start again. In such circumstances I believe that divorce is the action of Christian love, for I do not think that Jesus would have insisted that two utterly incompatible people should be condemned to drag out a loveless existence, heartbreaking for themselves and disastrous for their children. Nor do I believe that they should be forbidden to remarry and to remarry with the blessing of the church. Nor do I think that I would wish to talk much about innocent and not innocent parties, for when a marriage breaks up I should doubt if there is any such thing as an altogether innocent and an altogether guilty party.

iii. But now we must come to what is the most difficult side of this whole matter. What has the Christian ethic to say about sexual intercourse before and outside marriage? I think that the situation in regard to sexual intercourse before marriage is more difficult today than it has ever been in history. For that difficulty there are certain reasons.

(a) There is first of all the quite simple fact that the voices which once spoke for chastity no longer do so. Joseph Fletcher, the Christian occupant of a Chair of Christian Ethics in America writes: 'The cult of virginity seems to me to be making its last stand against the sexual freedom which medicine has now made possible' (*Dialogues in Medicine and Theology*, ed. Dale White, p. 141). 'A growing number of church people', he says, 'are challenging fixed moral principles or rules about sex or anything else.' So virginity was only a cult, and is now a doomed cult, and men like Fletcher accept this as inevitable. In 1959 the British Medical Association published a handbook, entitled *Getting Married*, written by Eustace Chesser and Winifred de Kok, and in it there was the following sentence: 'Chastity is outmoded and should no longer be taught to young people.' It is true that in 1959 there were so many protests that the book had to be withdrawn, but the significant thing is that it got to the length of being published at all. One of the very significant things today is that, if we may put it so, the defences are being breached from the inside.

(b) There are certain physical facts in the situation. Two facts have come together to form an explosive combination. People mature much more quickly today. Fifty years ago the average age of the beginning of menstruation was seventeen; today it is thirteen. Further, marriage has to be delayed in many cases today, and, when a man is at his most sexually dynamic, he may be a student on a long course which to say the least of it makes marriage imprudent. This is to say that there is the dangerous situation that sexual maturity is earlier and marriage is later.

(c) Third, there are the enormous changes in the methods of contraception and the efficacy of these methods. In this country it was not until 1877 that the thing became an issue at all. In that year Charles Bradlaugh and Mrs Annie Besant published an elementary manual of birth-control and were promptly prosecuted and found guilty, although the verdict was reversed on a legal technicality. It was not until 1921 that the first birth-control clinic was opened at Walworth; it was not until 1930 that the first Ministry of Health clinic was opened, and it was not until 1934 that information was offered, and it was offered only to women suffering from abnormal conditions. This is to say it was not until 1934—and that is a year after I began in the ministry—that birth-control methods were made at all public and then only in the most limited way.

Contraception found its peak in the pill, which is easy to take, normally safe in action and almost infallible in effect. The methods of contraception have been so refined and rendered so effective that it is now not necessary for anyone to have a baby unless they want to.

(d) There is the astonishing prevalence of abortion. Throughout the world there is the incredible number of 30,000,000 abortions per year. Even in this country there are perhaps about 160,000. It is a staggering fact that in countries like Belgium and West Germany, which have so-called liberal abortion laws, twice as many babies are aborted as are born. Fletcher has gone to the length of saying that he would wish to see the day when no unwanted and no unintended baby was born (J. Fletcher, *Situation Ethics* p. 39).

(e) There is the enacting of increasingly permissive legislation. There is, for instance, the legislation which permits homosexual practices between consenting adults. There is the easing of divorce; and there was the suggestion that married grants should be extended to students who live together without being married. There is the enacting of legislation which makes it easier to do the wrong thing—and that is always dangerous.

As Fletcher has pointed out, in the old days there were three fears which went far to keeping a grip of sexual intercourse before and outside marriage—the fear of detection, the fear of infection, and the fear of conception (J. Fletcher, *Moral Responsibility*, pp. 88, 89). The fear of conception is taken away by the new methods; the fear of infection—so it is believed—is taken away by the new antibiotics; and the fear of detection will become less and less when the consequences seem less and less serious.

It is then clear that for the modern young person Christian chastity is much more difficult than once it was. What makes the situation much harder is that the church is not speaking with one voice on this. Fletcher quotes the case of Professor Leo Koch of Illinois University. Koch was a biologist and in 1960 Koch was dismissed for saying that premarital intercourse was ethically justifiable. What Koch said was this:

> With modern contraceptives and medical advice readily available at the nearest drugstore, or at least a family physician, there is no valid reason why sexual intercourse

should not be condoned among those sufficiently mature to engage in it without social consequences and without violating their own codes of morality and ethics (J. Fletcher, *Moral Responsibility* pp. 128, 129).

And that is Fletcher's own point of view—the point of view of a Professor of Christian Ethics. It would be easy to ask Fletcher to be a little more definite and accurate. What does he mean by *mature*? It is obviously impossible to measure maturity by age. There are many people, who by their birth certificate ought to be mature, and who in fact are unstable, impulsive, insecure and neurotic. One would like Fletcher to define a little more clearly what he means by *by consent*, for it is the most obvious thing in the world that it is not difficult to buy consent. What sounds so straightforward and obvious is in fact full of difficulties.

What then are we to say to all this?

i. In the first place, such sexual permissiveness is in fact fraught with very gráve danger. The facts are alarming. There are more than 150,000 new cases of venereal disease every year. In one year 37 young people under fourteen contracted venereal disease, as did 235 who were fifteen, and 1,357 who were sixteen. It is further to be noted that the fear of infection has returned, for some of the antibiotics formerly used are no longer effective, because strains of disease resistant to them have emerged.

It is further estimated that of boys of seventeen 1 in 4 has had sexual experience, and of girls of the same age 1 in 8; of boys of nineteen 1 in 3 has had sexual experience and of girls of the same age 1 in 4. Two out of three babies born to girls under twenty are conceived out of wedlock. Every thirteenth child to be born is illegitimate. In certain areas it is calculated that two out of three girls who have reached the age of twenty-five are no longer virgins. It is estimated that from 4 per cent to 6 per cent of men are practising homosexuals and the same percentage of women are lesbians. The divorce rate is running at over 40,000 divorces per year, and in the United States 1 in 4 marriages ends in divorce.

These are alarming figures. Permissiveness may be right, or permissiveness may be wrong, but quite certainly it is dangerous—and that is a basic fact not to be forgotten.

ii. No one can study the teaching of Jesus and of the New Testament without seeing that that teaching stands for purity and chastity. Fornication, which is sexual intercourse between unmarried people, is condemned at least eighteen times. It is one of the basic demands on the Gentiles that they do not practise it (Acts 15.20). It is not even to be thought of or spoken of by the Christian (I Corinthians 6.18; Ephesians 6.3). Adultery, which is sexual intercourse with a married person other than one's own marriage partner, is condemned at least fifteen times. In Jesus' words it is one of the sins which comes from the evil of the heart (Matthew 15.14).

Often the story of the woman taken in adultery (John 8.1-11) is cited as an example of the gentleness of Jesus, and from one point of view so it is. But how does it end? It ends by Jesus saying: 'Go, and *sin no more.*' There is no question of Jesus saying: 'It's quite all right. Don't worry.' There is no question of the woman getting the impression that the whole thing did not matter very much, and that forgiveness was easy to come by, and that she could easily do it again. The demand is: '*Sin no more.*' He leaves us in no doubt that he believed that she had sinned. She was forgiven—but she was firmly told that it must never happen again.

There is no way of making Jesus a supporter of a permissive society. If we support sexual intercourse before marriage or outside marriage, then I do not see how we can continue to call ourselves Christian, for a man cannot be a Christian and flatly contradict the teaching of Jesus Christ. It is one thing honestly to say that we will abandon the demands of Christian morality; it is quite another thing to abandon them and to deceive ourselves into thinking that we are still keeping them.

iii. It is for this reason that while it is right to stress the dangers of the permissive society, the argument from danger is not in itself a good argument, because it seems to imply that, if the danger could be removed, if there was no risk of a child, and no peril of infection, then the objection would be removed too. It tends to imply that the objection is to the attendant dangers and not to the thing itself. But, if sexual intercourse before and outside marriage is against the teaching of Jesus, then the thing is not only dangerous, it is wrong in itself—and that is what we are arguing.

iv. Let us go on with the argument. The supporters of the new morality place great stress on the fact that, as they put it, sexual intercourse has two functions—baby-making and love-making. They then argue that, since modern methods of contraception, especially the pill, have next to completely eliminated the production of a child, then there is no reason why the sexual act should not be used as love-making between people who are in love, but who are not married.

v. We may take in here something else with which few will disagree. Beyond all argument the Christian ethic teaches that it is always wrong to use a person as a thing; it is always wrong to use a person simply as the means of gratification or as a way of getting pleasure. Therefore, any act of sexual intercourse which is nothing other than the satisfaction of sexual desire is essentially wrong. That is why a marriage which is based on no more than desire is bound to fail, for the partners in it are basically using each other as things, and not as persons.

vi. Now we come to what is almost the final step in the argument. The sexual act is in the literal sense of the word *unique*. It is unique for two reasons. First, it has a unique potentiality, because through it a child, a new life, can be brought into the world. Second, it is unique, because it does something physically to a woman which cannot be undone, and which means that she literally will never be the same again. The breaking of the hymen is an irreversible fact. This means that there is no comparison whatever between an act of sexual intercourse and, say, a kiss. This is love-making of a different kind, love-making with a unique potential and love-making with a unique effect.

It can be said to be love-making at its peak. And such love-making ought only to be engaged in when people are totally, completely and utterly committed to each other. It can only rightly happen when people are so totally committed to each other that they have become one new person (Genesis 2.24; Matthew 19.5). The Old Testament uses the verb *to know* for the act of sexual intercourse. Adam knew Eve (Genesis 4.1). It is an act of complete and total mutual knowledge which can come only with complete and total self-giving. If it is less than that, it is not so much wrong as tragically less than what it ought to be. It is not the expression of a moment of passion, however intense; it is the expression of a permanent commitment, and only the willingness to enter into commitment gives the right to enter upon that unique act.

It could be put in this way. Whatever we say about the two functions of sexual intercourse, the love-making and the baby-making, it remains true that the biological reason for the sex instinct is the begetting of a child. That is why it was ever given to us. This is the very economy and arrangement of nature. Therefore, even when it is an act of love-making, it may properly only be engaged in by those who would gladly and willingly use it to beget a child, even although at that particular moment it is not their intention to do so. It is the expression of a commitment of which a child is the symbol and the proof.

★ It thus becomes clear that the great fault of premarital sexual intercourse is quite simply that it demands privilege without responsibility; it demands rights without commitment. This is why sexual intercourse is wrong even between people who say that they are so much in love that marriage is certain and that they are only anticipating what will in any event happen. We know too well how in the uncertainty of life even such a love can somehow find an interruption and even such an anticipated marriage may not take place. The utter commitment is still not entered on and therefore the unique act is wrong. The ultimate commitment must be fully there before the ultimate privilege is given and taken. Even if such a view involves self-discipline, it leads to the deepest satisfaction in the end. There is something tragic in making that which is sacred commonplace, and that which is unique ordinary. There are things—and these the greatest things— whose value only fully comes when we do not take them until the time to take them has fully come.

There are still certain other things to say. There are few nowadays, except in the Roman Catholic church, who would question the use of methods of birth-control within marriage. No one would wish to go back to the nineteenth century, when Charles Dickens' wife, before he left her, had ten children and five miscarriages in rather less than twenty years. But today the problem faces us as to whether methods of birth-control, and in particular the pill, are to be made available to those who are not married. We have already made it clear that we believe that for the Christian who will accept the Christian ethic sexual intercourse before and out-side marriage is wrong. For the Christian, therefore, the question does not arise. The Christian girl will neither want nor use the pill before marriage. But, if a girl were to come to me, and if she quite deliberately refused to accept the Christian ethic of sex, if she said that she intended to have sexual inter-course before marriage, I would argue with her, I would plead with her, I would pray with her, I would do all that I possibly could to persuade her to accept the Christian way. But if at the end of the day she would not listen, if no matter what I or anyone else said, she insisted on going her own way, then I would make the pill available to her, for I think that anything is better than to bring into the world an unwanted child. I think that those who oppose this are often illogical, for such people do not often insist that the older-fashioned instruments of birth-control should be withheld from the unmarried. In principle, there is no difference at all. If one is withheld, all should be withheld. But, if I cared deeply for someone, and if in spite of all I could say that someone refused to accept the Christian view of sex, and proposed to engage on it before marriage, I would wish to do all I could to save her and to save the child who might be born from the tragic consequences which could arise, and for that reason I should make the best methods of birth-control available to her.

It is hardly possible to leave this subject without a word about sex education. It is here that Christianity got off to a bad start. We have already had occasion to mention Gnosticism, which was a way of thought deeply ingrained into the Greek mind. It came from a deep suspicion of the body, and from the idea that, if a man could only be freed from the body, life's problems would be solved. It painted a picture of a world which from the beginning had been made out of bad stuff. It did not think of a world made from nothing, but a world made from material which in its very essence was faulty. Of such a world the true God could not be the creator, and so the Gnostics believed the world to have been made by an inferior god, ignorant of, and hostile to, the true God. If that is believed, then the world and all that is in it become evil. If matter is evil as such, then the body is evil as such. And if the body is evil as such, then all the body's instincts, and especially the sex instinct, are evil. This was originally a heresy, but it left its mark on the Christian church. Always the church has been suspicious of the body, and therefore sex has always been looked on as a kind of wicked thing. This meant that it was never spoken of; it was a kind of unfortunate necessity. There never was any sex teaching, for sex was something at best to be whispered about in corners, or to be made the subject of a smutty joke. This attitude still lingers.

It always was a wrong attitude, and today it is not only wrong, it is also highly dangerous. The sex instinct is a God-given instinct, implanted in us by the Creator. It is something entirely natural, and an integral part of human life.

Knowledge of sex must be taught. It must be taught quite objectively. Its mechanism must be taught, for only then will its dangers and its glories be realised. It is high time that the day when young people got their knowledge of sex through furtive whispered conversations and through dirty stories came to an end.

It will, I believe, better be taught on two levels. On the physical level it will be better taught at school, for often the teacher can speak freely of that which is embarrassing to the parent, and there are some things which are more easily taught in a group. Factually the school is the place for the teaching of sex. But the home is the place where the greatness of purity and chastity and fidelity can alone be taught. Let the school teach the facts, and let the home teach the ideals. It need not be an exclusive division. Often the good teacher will transmit the ideal, and often the good parent will already have talked with the child. But here is somewhere where school and parent can really co-operate.

It is often objected that the child will try to experiment with the new knowledge that he has gained. For a few years it could be so, for at the moment we have not yet escaped from the situation in which that which has been so long secret is being unveiled. But, given time, and no very long time will be necessary, such teaching will become a normal part of the child's life in which healthy knowledge will take the place of unhealthy curiosity, and there will be a far better base to build on, a base in which the dangers are known, the facts realised, and, if we teach rightly, the ideals glimpsed.

If ever there was a time to uphold the standards of the Christian person to person ethic this is it. It is now that the Christian light should be shining like a light in a dark place. The plain fact is that the church has lost the very reason for its existence, if it pursues a policy of conformity to the world.

The world wants the church to be the church. Some years ago *Punch* had a cartoon. It showed the padre walking out of an RAF mess, leaving two officers behind. The one officer turns to the other and says: 'I can't stand this unholier than thou attitude.' The world may not agree with a church that insists on being different—but it will respect it. But it will have neither respect nor use for a church which is always trying to conform to the world. B. K. Price writes: 'The Swedish Lutheran church is to set up a special commission to reconsider a pronouncement made in 1959 which branded premarital sexual relationships as sin. A spokesman said that the commission would study whether this pronouncement should be modified in view of a widely-discussed demand that the church align itself more closely to "reality" ' (R. H. Fuller and B. K. Price, *Christianity and the Affluent Society*, p. 116). Fuller and Price were writing in 1966, and I do not know the result and verdict of the commission; but to align the church to the world, in the name of aligning it to reality, is the quickest way to suicide for the church.

There is a letter from C. S. Lewis to his brother (*Letters of C. S. Lewis*, ed. W. H. Lewis, p. 177) in which Lewis tells of a visit to Oxford of Charles Williams. Williams was a close friend of Lewis, and Williams fanatically loved and worshipped purity: Lewis writes:

On Monday Charles Williams lectured, nominally on *Comus*, but really on chastity. Simply as criticism it was superb—because here was a man who really cared with every fibre of his being about 'the sage and serious doctrine of virginity', which it would never occur to the ordinary modern critic to take seriously. But it was more important still as a sermon. It was a beautiful sight to see a whole roomful of modern young men and women sitting in the absolute silence that can *not* be faked, very puzzled but spellbound . . . What a wonderful power is the direct appeal which disregards the temporary climate. I wonder if it is the case that the man who has the audacity to get up in any corrupt society and squarely preach justice or valour or the like always wins?'

It may be that what the church needs to get the people back is not compromise, but a message of uncompromising purity.

Bibliography

This is not intended to be a complete bibliography. I have only listed the books which have been specially helpful to me in the preparation of these lectures.

ALEXANDER, A. B. D.: *Christianity and Ethics:* Duckworth, London, 1914
The Ethics of St. Paul: James Maclehose and Son, Glasgow, 1910

ALLAN, D. J.: *The Philosophy of Aristotle:* Home University Library, Oxford, 1952; Oxford Paperback University Series, 1970; Oxford University Press, New York (paper)

ARMSTRONG, A. H.: *An Introduction to Ancient Philosophy:* Methuen and Co. Ltd., London, 1947; University Paperbacks, 1965; Beacon Press, Boston (paper)

ATKINSON, R. F.: *Conduct, an Introduction to Moral Philosophy:* Basic Books in Education, Macmillan, London, 1969

BARKER, C. J.: *The Way of Life:* Lutterworth Press, London, 1946

BARNES, KENNETH C.: *He and She:* Darwen Finlayson, Beaconsfield, Bucks, 1958; Penguin Books, Harmondsworth, 1962

BARRY, F. R.: *Christian Ethics and Secular Society*: Hodder and Stoughton, London, 1966

BONHOEFFER, D.: *The Cost of Discipleship,* tr. R. H. Fuller: SCM Press Ltd., London, 1948; Macmillan Company, New York

Ethics, ed. E. Bethge: SCM Press Ltd., London, 1955; Macmillan Company, New York

VAN BUREN, PAUL: *The Secular Meaning of the Gospel;* SCM Press Ltd., London, 1963; Macmillan Company, New York

CARY, M. AND HAARHOFF, T. J.: *Life and Thought in the Greek and Roman World:* Methuen and Co. Ltd., London, 1940; University Paperbacks, 1961; Barnes & Noble, Inc., New York

CATHERWOOD, H. F. A.: *The Christian Citizen:* Hodder and Stoughton, London, 1969

CAVE, S.: *The Christian Way:* James Nisbet and Co., London, 1949

DEMANT, V. A.: *An Exposition of Christian Sex Ethics:* Hodder and Stoughton, London, 1963

DEWAR, L. AND HUDSON, C. H.: *Christian Morals, a Study in first Principles:* University of London Press Ltd., Hodder and Stoughton, London 1945

DOWNIE, R. S. AND TELFER, ELIZABETH: *Respect for Persons:* George Allen and Unwin Ltd., London, 1969; Schocken Books, Inc., New York

EARP, F. R.: *The Way of the Greeks:* Oxford University Press, London, 1929; AMS Press, New York

EWING, A. C.: *Ethics:* The Teach Yourself Books, English Universities Press Ltd., London, 1953; Free Press, New York

FERGUSON, J.: *Moral Values in the Ancient World:* Methuen and Co. Ltd., London, 1958; Fernhill House, Ltd., New York

FIELD, G. C.: *Plato and his Contemporaries:* Methuen and Co. Ltd., London, 1930; University Paperbacks, 1967; Barnes and Noble, Inc.

FLETCHER, J.: *Situation Ethics:* SCM Press, Ltd., London, 1966; Westminster Press, Philadelphia
Moral Responsibility: SCM Press Ltd., London, 1967; Westminster Press, Philadelphia

FLEW, R. NEWTON: *Jesus and his Way:* Epworth Press, London, 1963; Alec R. Allenson, Inc., Naperville, Ill.

FOOT, PHILIPPA, ed: *Theories of Ethics:* Oxford Readings in Philosophy, Oxford University Press, London and New York, 1967

FRANKENA, WILLIAM K.: *Ethics:* Foundations of Philosophy series, Prentice-Hall Inc., Englewood Cliffs, New Jersey, USA, 1963

FULLER, R. H. AND RICE, B. K.: *Christianity and the Affluent Society:* Hodder and Stoughton, London, 1966; Wm. B. Eerdmans, Grand Rapids, Mich.

GALBRAITH, J. K.: *The Affluent Society:* Hamish Hamilton, London, 1958; Penguin Books, Harmondsworth, 1962; Houghton Mifflin Co., New York

HUBY, P.: *Greek Ethics:* New Studies in Ethics, Macmillan, London, 1967; St. Martin's Press, Inc., New York

HUDSON, W. H.: *Ethical Intuitionism:* New Studies in Ethics, Macmillan, London, 1967; St. Martin's Press, Inc., New York

HUTTON, M.: *The Greek Point of View:* Hodder and Stoughton, London, n.d.; Kennikat Press, Inc., Port Washington, N.Y.

INGE, W. R.: *Christian Ethics and Modern Problems:* Hodder and Stoughton, London, 1930; Greenwood Press, Inc., Westport, Conn.

JONES, W. H. S.: *Greek Morality in Relation to Institutions:* Blackie and Son Ltd., London, 1906

KAMENKA, E.: *Marxism and Ethics:* New Studies in Ethics, Macmillan, London, 1969; St. Martin's Press, Inc., New York (paper)

KEELING, M.: *Morals in a Free Society:* SCM Press Ltd., London, 1967

KNOX, J.: *The Ethic of Jesus in the Teaching of the Church:* Epworth Press, London, 1962; Abingdon Press, Nashville

LEHMANN, P. L.: *Ethics in a Christian Context:* SCM Press Ltd., London, 1963; Harper & Row, Inc., New York

LILLIE, W.: *An Introduction to Ethics:* Methuen and Co. Ltd., London, 1948; University Paperbacks, 1961; Barnes & Noble, Inc., New York
Studies in New Testament Ethics: Oliver and Boyd, Edinburgh and London, 1966

LODGE, R. C.: *The Philosophy of Plato:* Routledge and Kegan Paul, London, 1956; Humanities Press, Inc., New York

LONG, E. L.: *A Survey of Christian Ethics:* Oxford University Press, London and New York, 1967

MABBOTT, J. D.: *An Introduction to Ethics:* Hutchinson University Library, London, 1966; Doubleday & Co., Inc., New York

MACINTYRE, A.: *A Short History of Ethics:* Routledge and Kegan Paul Ltd., London, 1967; Macmillan Company, New York

MACKINNON, D. M., ROOT, H. E., MONTEFIORE, H. W., BURNABY, J.: *God, Sex and War:* Fontana Books, Collins, London, 1963

MACQUARRIE, JOHN: *Three Issues in Ethics:* SCM Press Ltd., London, 1970; Harper & Row, Inc., New York

MOORE, G. E.: *Ethics:* Home University Library, Oxford, 1911; Oxford Paperback University Series, Oxford, 1966; Oxford University Press, New York (cloth and paper)

NIEBUHR, REINHOLD: *Moral Man and Immoral Society:* Charles Scribner's Sons, New York, 1932; SCM Press Ltd., London, 1963

OUTKA, G. H. AND P. RAMSEY: *Norm and Context in Christian Ethics:* Charles Scribner's Sons, New York; SCM Press Ltd., London, 1968

PATON, H. J.: *The Moral Law, Kant's Groundwork of the Metaphysic of Morals,* translated and analyzed; Hutchinson University Library, London, 1948; Barnes & Noble, New York

PAUL, L.: *Coming to Terms with Sex:* Collins, London, 1969

RAMSEY, I. T., ed.: *Christian Ethics and Contemporary Philosophy:* SCM Press Ltd., London, 1966; Macmillan Company, New York

RAMSEY, P.: *Basic Christian Ethics:* Charles Scribner's Sons, New York, 1950
Deeds and Rules in Christian Ethics: Scottish Journal of Theology, Occasional Papers No. 11, 1965

RAMSEY, P., ed.: *Faith and Ethics:* Harper & Row, New York, 1957; Torchbook Series, 1965

RANKIN, H. D.: *Plato and the Individual:* Methuen and Co. Ltd., London, 1964; University Paperbacks, 1969; Barnes & Noble, Inc., New York

RHYMES, D.: *No New Morality:* Constable, London, 1964

RITCHIE, D. G.: *Plato:* T. and T. Clark, Edinburgh, 1902

ROBINSON, J. A. T.: *Christian Freedom in a Permissive Society:* SCM Press Ltd., London, 1970; Westminster Press, Philadelphia
Christian Morals Today: SCM Press Ltd., London, 1964; Westminster Press, Philadelphia

ROSS, W. D.: *Aristotle:* Methuen and Co. Ltd., London, 1923, 5th ed., 1949; Barnes & Noble, Inc., New York
The Right and the Good: Clarendon Press, Oxford, 1930; Oxford University Press, New York
Foundations of Ethics: Gifford Lectures, Aberdeen, 1935, 1936; Clarendon Press, Oxford, 1939

ROUBICZEK, P.: *Ethical Values in an Age of Science:* Cambridge University Press, London and New York, 1969

RUSSELL, B.: *Marriage and Morals:* George Allen and Unwin, London, 1929; Paperback University Books, 1961; Liveright Publishing Corporation, New York

SAUNDERS, J. L.: *Greek and Roman Philosophy after Aristotle:* Readings in the History of Philosophy Series, The Free Press, New York; Collier-Macmillan, London, 1966

SCHNACKENBURG, R.: *The Moral Teaching of the New Testament:* Herder and Herder, New York, 1965

SCOTT, E. F.: *The Ethical Teaching of Jesus:* The Macmillan Company, New York, 1924

SELBY-BIGGE, L. A.: *British Moralists:* Clarendon Press, Oxford, 1897; Dover Books, New York, 2 vols., paperback, 1965
Sex and Morality: A Report presented to the British Council of Churches, 1966; SCM Press Ltd., London, 1966

SINCLAIR, T. A.: *A History of Greek Political Thought:* Routledge and Kegan Paul, London, 1951, 2nd ed., 1967

TAYLOR, A. E.: *Plato, the Man and his Work:* Methuen and Co. Ltd., London, 1926; University Paperbacks, 1960; Barnes & Noble, Inc., New York
Aristotle: Thomas Nelson and Son Ltd., London, 1943; Dover Publications, Inc., New York (paper)

THIELICKE, H.: *The Ethics of Sex,* tr. J. W. Doberstein: James Clarke and Co. Ltd., London, 1964; Harper & Row, Inc., New York
Theological Ethics, vol. 1, *Foundations,* ed. W. H. Lazareth: A. and C. Black, London, 1968; Fortress Press, Philadelphia

VIDLER, A. R., ed.: *Soundings, Essays, concerning Christian Understanding:* Cambridge University Press, London and New York 1963

WADDAMS, H.: *A New Introduction to Moral Theology:* SCM Press Ltd., London, 1964, rev. ed., 1965; Seabury Press, Inc., New York

WALKER, K. and FLETCHER, P.: *Sex and Society:* Penguin Books, Harmondsworth, 1955

WALSH, J. J. and SHAPIRO, H. L.: *Aristotle's Ethics:* Wadsworth Studies in Philosophical Criticism, Wadsworth Publishing Co. Inc. Belmont, California, USA, 1967

WARNOCK, MARY: *Ethics since 1900:* Oxford University Press, London and New York; Home University Library, 1960; Oxford Paperbacks University Series, 1966

WHITE, D., ed.: *Dialogue in Medicine and Theology:* Abingdon Press, Nashville and New York, 1967

WILLEY, B.: *The English Moralists:* Chatto and Windus Ltd., London, 1964; University Paperbacks, Methuen and Co. Ltd., London, 1965; W. W. Norton and Company, Inc. New York

WINTER, G., ed.: *Social Ethics:* SCM Press Ltd., London, 1968; Harper & Row, Inc.